The Busy Mom's Guide to Slaying Ecommerce

How to Sell More Products WITHOUT Needing Another 24 Hours In Your Day

~

A book by: Andrea Thomas

Foreword by: Tesa Colvin, TV Show Host, Bestselling Author, and Award-Winning Publishing Consultant

Copyright

The Busy Mom's Guide to Slaying Ecommerce
How to Sell More Products WITHOUT Needing Another 24 Hours In
Your Day

DEDICATION

Women have been the quiet storm of change for centuries, sometimes causing a strong undercurrent - ripple effect seen for years to come. Other times it's a loud defining roar causing everyone to stand at attention.
No matter which is yours, pursue it.

Table of Content

ACKNOWLEDGEMENTS

Writing this book has been a true birth. It would be misleading to say this entrepreneurial journey has been easy or clearly drawn out. There are many times I wanted to throw in the towel to live a traditional life many have succeeded in several times over. A question I've had to answer on more than one occasion was to either live a comfortable, predictable life or pursue what I was designed to do. And figure it out.

Following my own path, owning up to my mistakes, reaching out for support as I reach my next goal. Rinse and Repeat

My successes aren't my own, but because of those who listened to my visions, challenged my thoughts, let me know when I was wrong and cheered me up after countless falls, and celebrated my wins.

To Brian, who started this journey alongside me, sharing his last name, not truly knowing how much living outside the box would change how we view life, challenge our perspectives and add more depth to what we do every day. Here's to our next adventure.

You are the concrete to my abstract.

Thank you for giving me space to be who God has designed me to be.

And to my extended parents, Nana & Pops. Thank you for being a strong foundation for your son and nothing but supportive for us.

To My Bigs & Littles. Brea, Brice, Bellamy, Brax, and Blaine, before I knew you, I was doing this for you.

You have special God-given gifts and a purpose that will show you how to help others. As you pursue it, view any failures as a stepping stone and success as fuel towards your next accomplishments.

To My Parents. Where do I begin? You have gifted me a childhood I appreciate even more as an adult and in parenthood each day. You continue to give me the tools to be great and have an insatiable desire to help me be my best. It is a joy to watch you as grandparents. The grandkids' smiles say it all.

I will always cherish each season of life, insight, wisdom, and guidance.

To My Sisters. The extremes of me. I am forever proud to be your sister and watch you evolve into the people you are today. I'm excited to see where your paths take you and be a part of each chapter of your lives. Thank you for all you do, your encouragement, patience, and understanding as I juggle 7 lives and 39 businesses.

To Tesa Colvin, who has been forever patient with me as I anchored myself through my writings. Thank you for your guidance, patience, and hard pushes to get this work out of my head and onto paper. You have given your best, and it shows.

Above all, thank you, God, for sending your Son when I, personally, had no true understanding of how much love and sacrifice it required and meant. Thank you for each day I get to see a glimpse more of it to share with the world.

FOREWORD

Making the decision to bet on yourself and your dreams can be stressful.

Building a business and balancing every other aspect of your life can test your faith, your family bond, and even your sanity. But it IS possible!

On my entrepreneurial journey, I've struggled to find the right strategies to get results, I've struggled to work on my goals consistently, and even to meet my family's needs (physical, emotional, time, etc.). But again I stress, it IS possible!

The key is to adopt and adapt strategies and resources that you can REALLY use to propel your business forward and really aligns with you while connecting you with people who need your products and services. The key is to replace the energetic tug of war going on between your reality and your vision for your family, life, and business. And again I say - it IS possible!

And now, thanks to Author Andrea Thomas, who was not only willing to have a REAL conversation about the frustrating rollercoaster ride of emotion, but also provide some amazing strategies for creating curating and connecting with the people who desperately need your e-commerce business to succeed (because what you provide impacts and improves their lives).

So get ready to tap into exactly what you need to restore your vision of your business AND run a profitable store without jeopardizing your sanity in the process.

~Tesa Colvin~
TV Show Host, Bestselling Author, and Award-Winning Publishing Consultant

GIVE YOURSELF GRACE

I just want to take a moment. I just want to take a quick moment because I am currently in the car running an errand, even added an errand just so I could take more time to talk to you - kid-free.

Simply because I had a couple of thoughts, and my thoughts are dedicated to where you are right now. I think there's a part of life where some things are in and out of control. And what I have found when it comes to business is we often ask ourselves, when is it our turn? And we look at other people's businesses, we see them being successful, we see them celebrating, we see. We see them on social media, TV, podcasts, in magazines, ads, and we're like, how are they doing all of this, and when is it going to be my turn? When do they have time to get all this done? Perhaps what you're really saying is, I want that success.

The answer is probably shocking or surprising, at least because the answer is simply that it IS your turn. When you say it is, it's your turn to get the level of business & sales you want. When you say it, it is when you make up in your mind that now is the time. And that's something that, perhaps, we want someone else to look us in the eye and wave a magic wand and say with a firm voice, "It's your time." All of a sudden you have sales your way coming your way left and right, your business went from $ to $8 figures in days. But the truth of the matter is each one of these businesses did something to create the sales. Often time it's not one thing.

We all want the silver bullet. What's the one thing to do to get sales? What's the one thing to do to get more traffic? What's the one thing to do to become more profitable? And the truth is, it's actually several things done strategically and consistently over a span of time. That's the beauty of this process. As much as we want it to happen quickly or even overnight, we don't want to be a one-hit-wonder.

That would crush my spirit because it was a fleeting moment. All of the hard work hitting a peak of success, then flat-lining moments later. It wasn't something that could be rinsed and repeated. For music, when one-hit-wonders occur, the artist didn't recognize the times changing, the environment, or even the era of music changed. They just didn't shift.

They didn't know how to shift in time to catch the wave — having their ear to the streets, taking note of their audience, having a pulse of the market around them. And the whole point of this journey is consistency, yet giving ourselves grace for trial and error figure things out.

And even though we have a blueprint, it's not exact. And so this is why it is several things being done consistently overtime to get you the results that you really want. So why do I say it's your time to get what you really want when you say it is? Because then you're ready to focus on and figure out the strategy to create your desired outcome.

It's your race, at your pace.

It's not going to look the same as everyone else. Matter of fact, it may feel like you're moving at a snail's pace in comparison because of the chaos happening behind the scenes. But what I've found, it doesn't take a lot to bypass others along the way, as long as you're staying in your own lane.

ANALYZE, DECIDE, THEN LEAP

Since we have some extra time, I'll share my beginning. I wasn't even thinking about being an entrepreneur. I was just minding my newly-married self. A remarkable wedding went down in the books in a small town. Within a few months, I was going to be a mom. Petrified, I had already spent my "big moment of the year" on getting married. I was not ready for another by becoming a mom. My life had just started to fall into place. My career had taken a beautiful turn to actually design within my architecture firm, and my married life was still in newlywed bliss, things I wanted to enjoy 'as is' a while longer. I knew kids were on the horizon but wasn't anticipating that day to be THE day. I was an emotional wreck, just thinking about adding a person, becoming a family. I wish I was the overly excited mom to be, loving every single idea of becoming a mom. When the idea finally clicked that I was bringing a child into the world, the was actually mine; I decided to take six months off work post-delivery to see what it was like to just be a mom.

When she was born, motherhood clicked. I can't describe it. Most of my worries about being a mom vanished. She was a person I was happy to take care of, but she was NOT an easy baby. (yes emphasis on the <u>not</u>)

We did the whole daycare tour - figuring out which daycare would be best for my daughter once I go back to work at the three-month mark. I just felt like the daycare would get to witness all of the new baby memories. Meanwhile, I'd be at work, and they're going to be able to see her do things first. At that point, I couldn't see myself giving this

7

up to go back to my previous life. It's too different now. I have someone that's relying on me, and everything is different now. (Do you hear the music in the background? That could have been a song. I digress).

I spoke to my husband in what seemed like a circular conversation about should I stay, should I go. Finally, I made the decision to give up my career.

I remember a colleague of mine who worked part-time at our firm. I'd see her come in on time, do her work and leave on time with architecture, that was a strange sight to see. Unless we are dead on projects, we never leave. It must be written in the architecture code of honor book.

While the rest of us were burning the midnight oil, knee-deep in redlines, etching our voice inside the heads of our leads, raising our hands to get first dibs for new projects or roles, she would come in, do her work and leave on time.

It perplexed me so much, one day, I stopped by her desk to ask why she didn't have a visible drive or ambition to reach the next level in her career. I wasn't prepared for her blah answer. She replied to my question with such patience and said, "I'm content where I am. My family is more important than my career."

She was talking to a single, budding architect. None of this computed. Matter of fact, I was still confused at the end of our conversation. I couldn't imagine going to a job, doing an excellent job, but never wanting to climb the corporate ladder.

After I had my own daughter, I flashed back to our conversation and knew - what she meant. I couldn't wrap my brain around it all, but something was changing.

To be honest, there was a part of me that found great significance in my career. Shifting from being a career woman to stay at home, mom would be a mental adjustment, although I found tremendous joy taking care of my daughter.

While my world changed in one aspect, my friends didn't. I had to figure out how to relate to them again, as so many things were drastically different for me. After all, once I got together with friends and colleagues, how would I contribute when we talk about work? I can only say I used to be an architect for so long. Or "I remember working on projects like that." I had to come to grips with a new question, do I want to be a 100% stay at home mom? And if so, how long?

 I hadn't come to the conclusion yet, but I knew I was starting my new normal.

What I didn't mention was my sweet baby girl had a skin condition that reared its' head around two months of age. Our pediatrician was telling me at two months of age that it couldn't be eczema. And actually, she's not really scratching herself. She's not really itching because the itch mechanism in the brain or itch sensation doesn't occur in children until six months. Meanwhile, I'm watching my daughter actively rubber head her forehead against the sheets repetitively to scratch the itch. But because the doctors were doctors, I believed & trusted them. At least in the beginning. Eventually, the doctors agreed with my diagnosis of eczema. I came into an awareness of how motherhood instincts can truly guide me. Her eczema required around the clock attention. It started off as a gentle roar, then quickly turned into a full-fledge war.

My career abruptly ended, I was going through a mild identity crisis, and my baby was not like babies on TV. You know the ones where they are sleeping peacefully or cooing during the day. She was screaming and crying day and night, and didn't like sleep, which meant I couldn't sleep.

I knew having kids meant sleepless nights, but nothing could prepare me for being awake to prevent her from scratching subconsciously in her sleep too. And she was scratching all of the time.

This wasn't a little patch of itchy skin; it was all of her joints, her entire scalp, and face. Her face was discolored, and her skin was always inflamed and red. Anytime she was unsupervised, she was ripping into her skin to scratch the bone-deep itch. Flash forward six months, and we can't even give her a bath without her trying to dig into her legs and arms or any exposed skin. Brian and I were on call day and night to save her skin. And when we didn't catch her, she'd damage the newly healed area...again.

There were no products to really help any of us stay sane. Traditional mittens flew off, extra-long socks inched their way off in minutes, and those bodysuits with the mittens attached were a complete joke, she'd find a way to get a couple of fingers free in minutes. No peace, no sleep, always on alert. Since there was no product, I came up with one and began drawing it in my head. I'd visualize it, make alterations, and adjust it in my imagination. I was okay with foregoing sleep as I wasn't really getting sleep anyway. So while I'm up at 3:00 AM I'm with my baby, I might as well be up, researching and getting this product together and working on the website and, and, and...

Here I am with an idea to create a product to help her knowing it could help others who were in the same situation I was in. I had to make a decision. Do I continue being a stay at home mom? Do I continue to be 100% mom & wife focused?

My own mother laid her career aside to be a stay at home mom & raise her children. She never looked back. And I could see myself doing that. But there were a lot of questions there.

Did she have any regrets? Did she feel as if a part of her missing? Did she feel fulfilled? Although she was happily raising her family, there was a portion of her that worked so hard to establish a career she'd never touch again.

I think deep down, I wondered if I'd lose myself in being a mom. Possibly looking up to see there was more to offer, more problems to solve, ideas to design, buildings to erect. I was not sure if motherhood was solely my path.

Me being me. As I was contemplating those thoughts, processing this new chapter, life didn't pause long enough for me to take a breath. I made a prototype for my daughter, Brea, to use because scratching skin off is so overrated. I hand sewed satin to mittens to give my girl relief and save her skin. If you're visualizing anything elaborate or beautiful, stop. These hands do not sew anything beyond a pillowcase or straight lines. I would eventually work with a professional to make official prototypes because pen and paper, hand stitching scraps of fabric together, could only get me so far.

Sewing skills aside, these prototypes are making an amazing difference for her skin as her fingers couldn't claw at her skin. I began contemplating, do I extend this idea to help others as well? My husband said, how can you not?

Shortly after ending my career, a new one in entrepreneurship surfaced, and so did a doubt. My time was dedicated to raising and rearing my daughter. I can't jump-start a business. Can I create this empire and give her what she needs too? Can I do both? The only way to figure it out was to try it. And that's a risk that I was willing to take.

So with the baby on my hip and a dream in my head with handmade, half sewn prototypes not knowing anything about business or manufacturing outside of textbook knowledge, I started. I was fearless. My husband saw me making some strides. I just looked at him one day, and I said, "You know, if I could hire you one day if I could retire you from your job, would you want to work with me?" Exploring the "what ifs" and possibilities, I refused to believe the lie of I cannot do both. That same lie would still pop up with each new child. Can I do this now; can I still grow this company?

And my answer is still the same. Yes. You'll just have to do it a bit differently.
Honestly, I had to simplify my business to create success within the short sprints of time I had.

There are always key elements for any business (online or not). We need traffic. We need something to sell. And ways to get our products seen in front of new groups of people. All to create a brand people want to order from over and over and over again.

In other words, once we have a product to sell, we need a platform, community, and collaborating channels to have consistent, growing sales.

 My whole point is, even though this may seem like you're at a fork in your road, it's time to make a decision. Travel the path that's comfortable or stretch yourself (your family, your skills, and all that comes with it) to build the brand you originally dreamt of.

 Maybe you started off as a hobby, and its' growth is starting to make you uncomfortable. Maybe your sales are great, but you're overworked, tired, and stressed out trying to multi-task being a wife, mom, and seller. Maybe you bought a business from someone else. It's generating a lot of revenue, but as soon as money comes in, it goes right back out. When you calculate the numbers, you're wondering if the dream is just that.

Now growth seems like more of a burden than a joy; every time you find a rhythm with your kids, a new milestone happens, and they change all over again. You've been trying to find out if sleep is really a friend or foe. Your office has overflowed into the living room as your packing & shipping station, and if your husband asks one more time if he's going to see dollar's fall from the sky from your boutique, you may implode.

Growth seems like a green curse word. Perhaps you'll tone it down a bit and get comfy here.

But have you ever thought about this?

What if…. your product is THE solution to someone else's problem. And without your products on the market, that same person, your customer will not have your solution to solve it.

It sounds like I'm exaggerating, but if you think about it. I'm not.

Every business attracts a certain type of customer.

Your ideal customer.

Even if your competitor sells the same exact product, they're not attracting your customers. They are attracting their own customers. While some overlap, many don't. Matter of fact, your customer may not even realize this same product is the solution; without you guiding them towards it.

Somehow in the midst of the "building the business" part, our original mission got lost or buried in the packing and shipping, customer service, product curation, midnight nursing, 2am potty break, 5am email responses, 7:25am school and work handoff, and 4pm sports-dinner-bed combo.

So how do we pivot in how we run a boutique and ensure that it gives more than it drains?
It's simple, give more answers than questions.

What are the proper steps? If any?

Those proper steps are what I call my 3 Point Focus or in lament terms "Me, Us, Them." Your platform/conversions, your community, and collaborating channels. Don't let this 3 point focus fool you. It packs a hefty punch, AND it's meant to be simple to get rid of the overwhelm of building. This requires us to understand me: your platform, where the sales & conversions flow through, Us: our community (how they think, breathe and function) Before you think "Them" is a bad thing, it's simply knowing there's no need to do it all yourself, matter of fact it's ingenious to share audiences that are likeminded, collaborate with others to sell more. There's a joy in being able to sell on your website and social media and on someone else's piece of the internet. Sales can indeed flow all day every day with the 3 Point Focus in place. Whenever you're selling on a third-party platform, you are, in fact, collaborating to share their customers by giving them a piece of the sales.

So I pause for this question: when is it your time to make the sales you really want? When you say it is. Sounds easy, yet how do you go about this? It starts by letting this thought sink in. You are someone else's solution. The more you teeter-totter back and forth, should I put the time and energy in this? Should I not, should I hang this up to dry, or should I go for it full wholeheartedly? Should I pause and wait for the kids to grow up? Should I do it while the kids are little while I'm still growing our family? While the house is still a wreck, should I do this? Then ponder on if you want your products to be someone else's solution? What would those same people do without your products? Now I'll keep saying this, you designed your product for a reason, and it is not to stay in your head or in boxes on shelves, it's to be used by people who need them. And what better way to be someone else's solution than to sell your product to them?

So that is why you have to know your "why." Why are you doing this? If you're doing this to make money, that is going to fizzle. I'm going to just go ahead and say like, yes, money is one of the motivators, but it is not the key motivator.

With cuddling moments dwindling, you'll want to pause time to focus on your kids, yet knowing packing & shipping awaits or there's a conference call with a little one tugging on your pants wanting to color. Money won't matter, then, but your why will. And when you pair your "why" with a solid strategy, that's when the magic happens because this is bigger than you.

More than having enough money for your kid's college tuition or extra money for the kid's clothes and Starbucks Or paying bills or getting out of debt. This is about someone else. This is about your mission.

Helping someone else to live a fuller life because they were able to buy from your brand. I know, sounds a little woo, but it's important. I did not start ScratchMeNot to make money, money came because I was trying to fulfill a need. It helped my family first. And then I knew there were other parents like me suffering through the same situation. Parents and kids alike having sleepless nights who needed relief — googling at 3:00AM (because they're up anyway) searching for a true

15

fix, cure, anything to give the family peace. The list goes on and on. And so I filled the gap. The more people I find to help, the more it grows. I'm able to monetize on it in several different ways because I made sure my why stayed the main drive.

Don't get me wrong, the money makes a difference because no one wants to work for free, 365 days of the year. And that's why I focused on profitability because we have to have a bit of reciprocity, right? We have to feel like the time and energy that we're putting into this, all these dollars coming in that we actually get to keep some of it.

I'm not a proponent of running a business with the primary purpose is to make money. When the pressures of business surfaces, it's easier to bail. How you handle the days, the weeks, the time with low sales predicates, or dictates how you'll handle the time with high sales.

This is key.

How much you are committed to your business truly comes out when sales are low. Let me repeat that. How much you are committed to your business comes out when your sales are low. When sales are great, things are going good, it's easy to overlook the flaws as money hides it. With enough money to pay the bills, and a little bit of profit leftover, sales keep moving masking the flaws in your business.

But when one of the cogs in your store breaks, the facade starts to crumble, exposing our weaknesses. With the right systems in place, it makes the come up that much sweeter.

When I was growing up, I was taught when it comes to money, be a good steward of it. Be a good steward of money. I'll just give an example. If you are a church-going person, you know that tithing is important. God has given us 100%, and the least we can do is give him 10% (surely you can give them more, but 10% minimum.)

Whenever money flows in, 90% we keep 10% we give. If we started this practice at the start of our first job, when we were making $300 a paycheck, by the time we're making $3,000 a check, it's easy to follow the same routine. Buttttt if we say to ourselves, I'm only making $300, I'll start tithing when I get my first professional job, when it's time to give $300 to God from the $3,000 check, we may start to second guess that decision. Perhaps keep it with, a bit of guilt, but move on and, eventually, rarely tithe consistently.

What does tithing have to do with your store? This same concept holds true. Commitment

But what about the in-between time. The place you're in right now that's causing you to second guess what you've done thus far. You can't see the forest for the big tree in front of you. It's my "why" for writing this book because I remember looking at that BIG tree for so long it began to skew reality.

Obstacles that pop up make us think that our goals are unattainable when they are, they make us feel like we're not capable of handling, balancing our life, home, kids, spouse, husband, and work because these same obstacles seem so real and so big at this present moment we must stop everything to focus on them. But if you're able to zoom out, if you're able to say, okay, you know what, things are not aligned, but let me just take a moment and look at what I have accomplished, what I have done to see where I've come from to gain perspective on obstacles at hand.

::Pause here and let those memories flood your system::

The moment your product idea came to life. The second you decided to "just do it." To your first, second, third sale and seeing money (that's not yours) flowing into your bank account. Can you feel the excitement? Take a look at your very beginning and look at where you are now. It may not seem like large leaps, but they're coming. Your today may not feel as drastic as going from $0 to $1 million in sales in a year, but it can be. You're just in the middle of the beginning of your journey. Because depending on how long you do this, how far you want to take it , whether you want to be a mogul mom or a mom that happens to own a business, brings out how determined you are to figure this business thing out. Grab ahold of our emotions, look them in the heart, and let them know we're not at the end of our ropes. We're figuring out how to let this be easy.

So for our kids watching over our shoulders, for our husbands who believe in us, but not quite convinced it'll work, for ourselves as we look cluelessly at this tree, celebrate what you've done so far, congratulate yourself for taking the leap and giving yourself room and grace to figure this out.

Envision where you're going in vision, the possibilities, and the opportunity of your family getting a chance to glean and see you grow through it. And if I know only one thing about kids, they do what we do, not what we say. Ha! Your little ones are learning vicariously through us. Usually, they are the risk-takers. Flipping off sofas, trying to touch a hot stove, skating in a bag of flour on the floor...and rightfully so, the way kids learn is by doing, even if it doesn't make sense to their parents. Why aren't those things risky to us? Because we've lived enough life to know the outcome. You know what? It's your turn to be the risk-taker. Test out new waters, fall down, get up with an audience (your kids and spouse) watching. Ideally, we want to do this in a bubble all alone to avoid any humiliation or get unsolicited opinions / advice. BUT their cheers won't match your journey. So I'll say this plain and simple. Take risks boldly, have fun, go against the grain, fall, get up and try again. When the tree starts to take over the forest, zoom out. Celebrate your journey thus far, and the tree will shrink to its actual size. Yes, it's still an obstacle. It'll be one you can conquer. It can be freeing.

There's one thing I didn't mention. As you look at the trees in life (business aside), how are you showing up? How we show up in everyday life reflects in our business. How you show up when your kids are going crazy, and the house is absolutely unrecognizable, and your husband comes home, walks in, and immediately walks back out the door to check the address. Then perhaps asks the WRONG question, "What did you do all day?"

You guessed it, it reflects in our business. Our business is a reflection of us. It's a mirror. And sometimes when we simply don't like what we're staring at. It's at that moment that we decide to pivot or to stay in place. I say pivot, but I can't make that decision for you. If you don't like where you are, and you know where you want to go. Shift. Perhaps you've hit your sales ceiling. You've gotten used to your usual numbers. So when life happens, you may wonder, is this even worth it anymore?

I ask this in return. What do you really want? What is your ultimate goal? What sets you on fire? What impact are you trying to create? When I hear my customers talking about how much of a lifesaver my product is. When I see little ones wearing the product smiling, when I hear the emotion in the mom's messages and voices, when I speak to them, telling me how much of a life-changer their child has experienced due to my product alone, that gets me fired up. That makes me excited. That's what keeps me going. It's not the dollars in the bank. The dollars will follow. It will follow if you focus on building your community and giving what they need, product plus a little something we like to call value.

If you have a community similar to mine, sometimes your customers just want support or a community to talk to. Create that. Sometimes your people are corky and funny, and they just want to laugh, give them opportunities to. After we give value, then sell them your product. We have to get creative to find ways to give value to our people. When it's time for potty training, what works for one child doesn't for the other. Turn on that creative brain, and we can get out of this thing clean, sane, and potty trained. Ooh, that rhymed. Ok, enough potty analogies. But it's the same thing with your audience how can you serve them and keep them coming back. Give, give, take.

The more we create a space for our customers just to be themselves, share, and absorb, the more we can highlight our products as a solution to their concerns. Then we begin to see the power of conversations. I can collaborate over here, share an audience over there. The world of more customers and selling opens up simply because we realize we can make a bigger impact when we stop doing it alone.

IT'S CHEAPER TO KEEP HER

The community is really the heartbeat of the business. We hear about it on the back end, the culture of the business (people), and the front end by being customer-centered (people). Whether grown by ads or referred by a friend of a friend, who are now they're peeking through your virtual store windows. What do you do with them?

There are three types of customers new, existing, and soon to be customers. Also known as prospects, visitors or incoming traffic, strangers dropping by for a quick visit. How long will you hold their attention, talk to them, and actually get them talking about will determine if you have a "buy and leave" culture or a "sit down, buy & let's chat about it" movement. The longer they stay, the more they buy-in.

::Pause::

By now, this may sound borderline calculated and cold. This isn't a book on staying a hobby and giving away all of your goods for free. How I wish we could and still have a business. Without sales and cash flow, the doors close. Joining the statistic of 30% of new businesses fail during the first two years of being open, 50% during the first five years, and 66% during the first 10. *ouch* so calculated we must be.

::Unpause::

The community we're discussing gives us an easy, natural way to get to know our customers better, hear their thoughts through their own words, and simply understand what makes them tick and what makes them smile, laugh, all the emotions catching them with their guards down. Perhaps your business is very techie, doesn't require emotion or all the feels, hone in on that. Feed them what they want more of, give them a reason to stay awhile or come back every day.

Where is this community container, or space where to actually engage with your people? For starters, your email. You're collecting all these email addresses from your customers, sending them shipping updates, but what are you sending them afterward? Time to dust off your email marketing tool and take a look at it from another angle. These aren't just "Thank you for your order" emails or for holiday sales. I would highly recommend a welcome sequence for new customers to give them a chance to get to know your brand voice through a series of 3-5 emails. I've seen some awesome email series, and I've read a few that made me unsubscribe in minutes. Five emails telling your 'why,' giving them a preview of what to expect from you, upcoming events, resources and more ways to buy. The sole purpose is to get them to read and open the next email. Russell Brunson gave me some inside tips on how to set them up, and the keyword is suspense - anticipation of what will be inside the next email.

I won't dive into the specifics on email psychology and set up, but I will say this. Always ask yourself, will the subject line make them curious enough to open it, will the content have them anxiously waiting for the next email or as my copy friend, Kate Doster would say "Copy so good, it'll have you licking the screen" And will the email give them 1 maybe 2 things to do right now. Those are signs of a good email. Need help on emails and copy, look up Russell or Kate or check out my black book of resources to get those emails flowing, opening, and converting.

Are you sending them emails they want to read? I'd revisit your topics of choice. I chose to talk about 3 different topics, I've seen others talk about anything from a pen to a puppy in the ER (everyday life) and somehow circle it back to what they are selling or leading to the sale. The key to this is you're warming them up for additional sales. You're taking a new customer leading them onto a path to become a repeat customer.

There was a line on a 90's sitcom called Martin. Over the top, funny comedy. From all of his characters, Otis was the funniest. Loved his line — "It's cheaper to keep her."

Otis had to let those young men know, once you find a good woman, it's cheaper to keep her. You do it by being making her feel special

— recap on love.

Boy meets girl.

Both decide if it's a match through day & night conversations and dates. Dates turn into love. Love into marriage.

To stop in the middle of this cycle means to start all over with a whole new person. Losing all the time, energy, and money spent on the previous person.

Just to do even more of the same to find, attract, date, and love again...hope it works out.

Or take the Otis' approach. Work hard at keeping the spark alive, find ways to make stay, and never slip on your game.
As flawed as Otis' infamous line is. It rings true.

'It's cheaper to keep her'

In his eyes, Ole Otis Supreme is a rich woman's lover and a poor woman's dream. And the women he woo'd agreed.

Look at your incoming traffic as people who want to feel like the only person you care about is them. These are the 20% of customers who keep your business flourishing by providing 80% of the sales. The 80% of one time buying customers are the ones we're constantly spending marketing dollars on to replenish and multiply. Because they still provide 20% of our sales. And 20% of $100,000 in sales is still $20,000. All three types of customers have their place, creating solid sales.

These percentages won't always be exact, but it shows us the power of truly connecting with our community.

Your welcome series helps you stay in contact with them and stay top of mind.

Kudos for Brunson opening my eyes to looking at my emails in a new light. Ask yourself, if I were to send all of my emails out back to back to my customers, would they Netflix binge on them or unsubscribe? Are they high drama with suspense or full of info your customers can't consume fast enough?

If your customers have sent your emails to a junk email account (You know that email account you use for all of your online purchases, so they won't clog up your "real" account — ha!), would your subject lines snag their attention? And since our day and age has internet ADD, once the email is opened, would it keep their attention long enough to click a button to buy more.

Many times, they freely gave us their email address so we can send them tracking information for their order, but they weren't expected (or maybe now they do) was an email every day from Buy, Buy Baby asking them to do just that.

One of the things that I loved about the show Scandal. They close one aspect of the storyline, and they opened up another at the same time. So it keeps you waiting for their next move. Giving you just enough closure, but adding a large dose of 'what if' and curiosity. That's the power of email marketing. It's what our email marketing tool was designed to do. Keep your customers opening your emails, reading, and buying.

Before you breathe another deep sigh because email isn't your thing, think about your the apps on your phone. We may delete games, and random apps to save space on our phone or declutter, but one thing we rarely, if ever, delete is our email app. Emails aren't dead. But bad emails are. Kate brought this to my attention, and I've held onto that thought every time I thought about avoiding emails. Emails gift us those "While you were sleeping" sales. If nothing else, at least have these two types of email sequences set up: Welcome & Abandoned cart series.

There are other containers or places we can hold space for our customers to hang out and talk: social media, Facebook, or Instagram. Just remember you're on borrowed land, and those followers are not yours until you snag their email or they become a customer. We'll dive into that in detail later.

For now, take a moment to evaluate. Are you on the social media platforms where your ideal customers are? If that's a checkmark, then we'll want to make sure this is not a one-way conversation. Post, give a call to action (something for them to do) and respond to them when they comment or like to keep the conversation going. Which, of course, keeps the sales flowing. Email is your one true asset. People inside of your Facebook group, people on Instagram, those are not your assets. They are not truly yours. When you have their email address. Now you have a proper way to talk directly to your customer. If Facebook or Instagram shuts down, if they block you, close your account, you'd have no access to that community. Because. You were on borrowed land.

Let's talk about creating a container, an asset that's actually yours. Those assets revolve around how you can reach them, email, phone, or address; each has its own pros and cons. This portion of your business is sellable in and of itself.

Beats by Dre anyone? In 2014, Apple purchased Beats by Dre, both the Beats Music and Beats Electronics for $3 Billion. Many thought it was because of their physical product - Beats Electronics — their headphones. They prided themselves on bringing "the energy, emotion, and excitement of playback in the recording studio to the listening experience,"; being a premium headset that not only looked good but went head to head with brands like Boise.

Visually and performance-wise, this headphone business aligned with Apple's brand, making it easy to understand why Apple would want to acquire it. Simple, sleek, high-quality electronics. The most we had at the time from Apple was their white wired earbuds.

But it was the digital asset, the community that Apple really had its eye on. Beats Music had a large playlist of curated music for its music subscription / membership platform. Now Apple already had a playlist and subscription but nothing in comparison. To a buyer's eye, this is also a list of customers, subscribers, and buyers. Apple wanted to expand its music platform. Beats had already done that for them. More importantly, Apple wanted to acquire a new group of paying customers. Again, Beats had already done that for them.

Those customers became Apple's.

Their customer's contact info: emails, addresses, phone numbers all were acquired as their own.

Years later, the headphones themselves are still selling. Notice how they didn't make any significant changes to them. Apple Music and its monthly membership have since exploded. Now that's the bankable asset, the gift that keeps on giving.

What are you creating that's sellable outside of your products? I hope you dropped what I was laying down. Save that one for future expansion.

For now, note your containers / community - Email, Phone, Addresses. How are you engaging with your potential customers and current customers to keep them engaged and buying? What's your exit strategy? Get acquired, purchase someone else's business? Hand it down to your children? Oooh, the smile on my face just got bigger.

So what about today, today is a great day to focus on strengthening your community-building it to the point of becoming a true viable multi-million or billion-dollar company and exit asset. Now that we've seen the aerial view of what we are creating long term, it's easier to see how emails social media posts and ads need to be anchored with measurable results today.

We often create campaigns to give us those results. According to Google, a campaign requires us to work in an organized and active way toward a particular goal.
Goal: X amount of traffic (x) product = X amount of sales

we have a product we want sales for. We find a group of people who may be interested in it (i.e., traffic), we position the product for sale (website), we show them other products people have seen (upsell), then give them space to check out. Rinse and repeat — split test.

The results you want dictate the campaign.

We analyze the results to decide if we want to scale it or turn it off and call it failed.

Did it take $100 to get $1000 in sales, or did it take $1000 to get $1000? — Both created sales. Yet it's easy to see which output was greater. I once turned off one of my BEST campaigns, simply because I didn't understand this concept. I was only focused on the sales the campaign created. Sounds the same, but hear me out.

The concept of selling products is simple, just like the formula I gave above.

Get a product, drive traffic to them, sell them, throw in an upsell or 2…rinse and repeat

As I was analyzing the results, I didn't understand what I was looking at.

When I was thinking of creating a campaign, brand influencers came to mind.

I've combed these Google streets searching for how to get more traffic, consistent buyers/customers.

I've watched YouTube like I was Netflix binging.

I had to figure out how it worked. I wasn't sure of my angle.

For my product, I sell to moms and dads.
(Did you catch my mistake?)

So I did an influencer campaign to moms and dads.

It failed.

I decided to think like my customer and came up with a CRAZY, great influencer campaign, with Doctors.

It wasn't crazy successful. The dollars weren't rolling in like those ads all the gurus on Facebook taught. But I was still getting more buyers than my previous campaign that tanked.

We did this for 1 quarter each year for 2 years.
(another mistake)

I looked at the sales and realized I wasn't getting enough return on the investment, time, and money. I made $500 off a $100 investment. What was $500 when I was making $5-10,000 in sales a month? $500 didn't seem like a lot considering my goals.

I stopped.

Looking back, I should have poured gasoline on that campaign and lit it with a blow torch.

It was my best campaign EVER at that time.
I'm a microwave girl at times, and if it doesn't produce big results fast, I end it.

What I didn't understand is this.

Anytime you put in $100, get back $500
That's a 5 ROI (Return on Investment) or ROAS (Return on Ad Spend) in the Ads world.

I was on to something, and I should have paused to scale it.

But all I could see was the measly $500.

One ads guru swears 1-4 ROAS (Put $1 and get $4) is the e-commerce industry average. I was at a 5, I was already killing it.

If I would have scaled:
Take $200, make $1000
Take $1000, turn it into $5000

The other said their goal is 5-6 ROAS; we turn off anything 4 or lower and scale to 10 or as high as it can go.

What does that have to do with my Doctor's campaign?

I was on to something and had no one to run these thoughts by to confirm or deny my findings.

Even putting in a dollar and getting a dollar - Breaking even has its place.
IF you upsell shortly after, you'll have a repeat customer you've only paid for once.
New customers are expensive, and we must focus on repeat sales for a firm foundation. Especially in eCommerce where the profit is thinner than service-based businesses

Had I known I was at a 5 ROI back then, I'd be screaming...cue the Simpson's, "Shut up and take my money."

Get comfortable analyzing the numbers. (or find someone who will break it down for you).How much in sales did it take to hit that number?
What, how many emails did it take to reach that?
Which split test is winning?

How much did we spend on shipping vs. manufacturing?
What's our peak selling season numbers vs. the remaining part of the year?
Do we have enough inventory on hand to beat last quarter's sales?

What do Beats by Dre, 5 ROAS campaign, and knowing your numbers have to do with community?

They all tell you the best places to build and grow your community based on conversions.

Last time I checked, Facebook had over a billion members constantly on Facebook checking for news, memes, and getting the scoop on their family and friends. You'll begin to notice the easiest place to build a community is by having a presence on a social media platform. If you tried to reach all 1 Billion, you'd run out of many and lose your mind quickly. The more time, energy, and money you invest in getting to know your audience, your people, the more money you'll make. The more lives you'll change with your products. The key to remember, whether you're on Facebook, Instagram or even Snapchat, remember you are now playing on someone else's turf.

You have to abide by their rules. I pause here to say, think like a customer, act like a business. Each platform dictates how and if you can sell your products, even if you can continue talking to your audience. So we're always looking at how I can get these potential customers off of social media and onto an email list, website, or anywhere that is on our own piece of the internet where we make the rules (ethically) and profit the most.

I have seen countless times where people are selling products on Facebook, even Etsy or Amazon, then violate their terms and conditions or rules unintentionally, getting themselves locked out of accounts. They get put into Facebook jail, their key accounts get closed. Even someone (usually a competitor) decides that they don't like them for whatever reason and reports them, and now their account is under review or suspended. Crazy things happen on 3rd party platforms. To protect ourselves, we stay in stealth mode to sell more products anywhere but direct our traffic to ourselves.

Can you imagine having a $100,000 business account closed in a matter of days because of the above?

It's very disruptive as it not only stops sales; it stops any and all conversations with your community. Now imagine having 483 customers you cannot talk to as your products collect dust on the shelves. You'll be forced to rebuild elsewhere until it's resolved or scramble for sales.

The next logical question is, how do I make the transition. How do I maximize social media and still drive sales to my website?
Keep it super simple, in 2 words.

Discount code.

It's a tried and true method of give and take. I'll give you 20% off IF you give me your email address.

Boom.

Done.

Who turns down 20% off? Matter of fact, customers will give 5 different emails to use the code again and again. ha! There are ways to prevent this, though, by using apps that track IP addresses to stop a customer from taking advantage.

The codes are an amazing way to get them involved in your world and get them attached to you or your brand. Another way is through a freebie they'd drop everything for, give them value in exchange for the email address, and sell to them through follow up emails. There are many other ways, yet these are two of the main, easiest ways to start. Once this is in place, we can breathe easy knowing the community we are building is truly ours.

The next question may seem obvious, but who are you selling to? Who's your product for? If you skip this step, you'll come back to it - After losing crazy money because you were trying to sell to a wider niche than necessary. Using your precious funds to market to people who will care less about your products.

Ouch

Let's keep those dollars cozy in your bank by figuring out who you're really selling to now.

WHAT IF YOUR IDEAL CUSTOMER ISN'T A PERSON?

When I first entered the eCommerce scene, we are taught that we are to embody a person and understand where they live, what they think, where they shop, how many kids they have. All of which creates a certain type of person then we market. Matter of fact, I use to take myself and my clients down this crazy long list of questions and dream of "describe your ideal customer" Is it a male or female, single or married, how many kids, middle high or low income, college graduate, mom of 5 or single dad of 1, senior dog lover?

Then I'd ask if they were single income or DINKs (Dual income no kids), do they drive a minivan or SUV, 2 cars or 4 cars, kids in college or newlyweds. And the list would go on and on.

Your ideal customer is what we are taught to focus all of our marketing efforts. We ensure that we are actively speaking their language, talking to them in a way that grabs their attention enough to buy our products. That's the real goal, right? When sitting down with our product, we ask ourselves, "Who is this product really for? How can I get this in front of them?"

With a list of demographics and questions, we're taught to create an avatar — an ideal customer to direct our marketing towards. We want to get inside their minds to draw them to us.

Now while all of these questions have meaning and are relevant to our ideal market, I was left with more questions because of this exhaustive list of demographics. Now what? Do I make up a fantasy lifestyle for her or him? Assign her 2.5 kids? Name the family or person who embodies the demographics? Take your imaginary family and add some pain points associated with your brand, now we have our business marketing angle.

And that also creates a lot of gaps to fill.

So, I'm going to challenge that, I'm going to ship that to the side, and we're going to really look at your ideal customer in a very, very different way. What if your ideal customer isn't really a person at all? Even with a perfectly orchestrated description of your customers, we still have to figure out their pain points and what makes them move to buy fast.

Block out referring to your avatar as a person; instead envision a golden trail, like the Wizard of Oz, as a series of events of each problem driving them to your solutions. As inventors or sellers, we understand their journey even more than they do. We spend countless hours dissecting their world to sell more products.

For ScratchMeNot, I make products for children who have eczema, hair pulling, things of that nature. Having been there done that with my own children, I know what it looks like when itchy skin is at its worst. I also know what it looks like on the other side of having clear skin and not having to worry about eczema. I have a well-rounded understand the journey, even though each person's journey has its own nuances, I know enough to fill in the gaps. As we speak to these customers, we'll be able to add more to this pain point timeline in their own words. Therefore, when speaking to my customers through my products, I am portraying that information to them.

I'm also causing my brand to be a magnet to where they come to me as we're leaving little breadcrumbs all over the internet back to the brand to learn more and/or purchase our products.

An avatar means nothing without a pain point timeline. Until this point, I had to stop looking at my ideal customer as a person with a set of demographics. When I look at the actual customers, they rarely match that person exactly. Yet, when I add the pain point timeline to the demographic questions asked before, it gives my marketing a solid opportunity to shorten the know, like, trust, buy factor.

Remember, I'm not the only one with a solution; there are creams available, other clothing available, etc. Being aware of this, I need to be able to reach them in the middle of their itchy skin journey, where they are, guiding them towards me — problem to solution vs. actual person.

The personification of this pain point journey is going to come in forms of people. The types of people who align with the original set of demographics. How does this work in real life?

I'm happy you asked. Athlete's foot powder. Random, off the top of my head. Let's roll with this product example. The athlete's foot powder is really designed to kill the bacteria. Kill what's living in that shoe, in that sock, on that foot, which then stops the itch and ultimately stops the smell or anything associated with the side effects of the condition.

That's from the benefit side of the product. Now, from the customer's side of their experience, all they're thinking is, "My foot itches, my shoes stink. My feet are burning, and I cannot stop this burning. I want to pull off my sock and shoe in the middle of a meeting and scratch excessively as if I'm the only person in the room. I need a solution for that."

So, if you come bouncing over to your customer, "Hey, here's our athlete's foot powder, it's going to kill the bacteria, the powder is so thin and smooth you'll barely notice it's there. And not only is the powder is odorless, but it also will not leave any residue," You're going to lose a lot of potential customers. At this point in their journey, they're thinking, "I have this crazy itch that's burning nonstop on my feet. I need to resolve that. Now my feet smell, causing me to leave a trail of stench behind." In the original marketing angle, none of his pain points were addressed, only the features of the product.

Instead of talking about how this product is going to kill the bacteria, we need to say, "You know what? Athlete Fighter - Itch Be Gone (our athlete's foot powder) is going to stop the burning, never-ending itch sensation, and ultimately end the stench." Now, their ears are open. Ready to buy, receive, and pray it actually does what you say.

Decide what advertising scenarios you'd like to focus on. "If your feet are burning, you just want to start raking your feet in the middle of a meeting, or you are embarrassed to go to karate class because all noses point to you. Our Athlete Fighter - Itch Be Gone powder is for you."

This is how we are meeting them where they are in their journey.

Now, take those same products at a different place in their journey. "My feet don't itch anymore; I've got that handled through the doctor's prescription. My favorite tennis shoes are under attack by my wife. I don't want to give them up, but I can't get rid of the smell left behind from the athlete's foot. She wants to throw them away because they smell so bad. I have 3 days to get this under control" A different place, pain is different, same pain point timeline. This person could be a male, it could be a female, it could be a child, it could be whoever, but the point is we are catching them on their emotional-physical journey.

The wife & stench are the pains. "Everywhere we go, she's embarrassed for (and of) me. But I don't want to get rid of them, and my feet smell. She hates these shoes."

It's time to tap into the problem gap and filled it with your solution. Especially the emotional side of why the itch or stench bothers the customer so much. This is what will drive him to take action of actually purchasing your product. Meet them where they are on their actual physical and emotional journey.

Our solution. "Athlete Fighter - Itch Be Gone doesn't just fight the itch; it gets rid of your shoe Oder in as little as 3 applications. Just sprinkle them in day and night for 3 days, eliminating the smell for good. No need to buy new shoes, use Athlete Fighter powder. Plus, you have our 30-day money-back guarantee."

All pain points addressed and confidence to move forward with the money-back guarantee. Depending on how far into our marketing cycle this potential customer is in, the more we educate to lead to the sale in the voice matching our ideal customer's demographics and how they communicate with us verbatim in our communities.

I got a little excited there, a little hopped up on avatars and pain point journeys because I wasted way too much time making up a fictitious character or family missing the mark in connecting with my potential customer. But when we pare it with our pain point timeline, we're able to get a full picture of how to socially sell on-demand - from emails to ads. Building momentum towards what I call sleep sales. Meaning, while you were sleeping, (pun intended) sales were flowing in when you weren't doing a thing — or playing with your kids. Or Netflix binging. Because you put in the right work now, you'll see the results that much faster.

YOUR CUSTOMERS NEEDS vs. WHAT THEY REALLY NEED

Depending on where you are in your business, you either came up with a product out of necessity, and you knew you could sell this product, but you may be having a hard time finding those customers. Or you may be the process of selling all over the place. Or maybe you have a whole series of questions or thoughts running through your mind.

I just don't know how to get my customers in my niche to purchase it. How do I know they actually need this product? We're going to break down these questions and more.

It comes down to thinking, understanding, and engaging, interacting with your ideal client. And so when I came up with the ScratchMeNot that I knew based on market research, my own personal experience, talking to others, how much people needed my product, everybody doesn't need my product.

This is a good thing. I learned to be ok with it. The number of people who do need my product showed me I could be a zillionaire if I reached every single one. So I pressed forward.

To be completely transparent, every single person in your niche will NOT see the need for your product. It's our job to share our products with our niche, and those it resonates with will move forward with the purchase. But no one will if we don't present our products for sale, to begin with.

There was an upcoming photoshoot for ScratchMeNot, and I was so focused on my niche, I was only looking for moms with children who experience itchy skin beyond the occasional scratch. This shoot was a dual purpose, to capture amazing photos, get some product testing and real-life testimonials under our belt. I was looking for parents of children who understood Eczema, either their children had it or experienced it to make it easier for them to feel comfortable wearing & using the products, both on and off camera.

One parent, in particular, whose child had mild Eczema. She took one look at my product, decided at that very second, "Oh, my child is not scratching to this degree!" It's not my first time dealing with rejection for my brand, yet it still stung more in person. I quickly reassured her it didn't matter, and I wanted someone with childhood eczema experience to use the product & review it. And for better, more natural movements on camera to show off the product's functionality.

She agreed to test it. A couple of weeks later, we did her interview. I was floored to hear how much she loved the product for her daughter. She was raving, talking on and on about the product.

She also took note as to how much her child was scratching in which she had become immune to hearing. Everything our product stood for, the reasons I designed and created it, to begin with, she was experiencing. The unexpected testimonial gave me a marketing 'ah-ha' moment. Even when people don't think they need your product, we just have to educate them more. First impressions are just that. Hence why it takes a person 7-21 times to see your products before it clicks for them to move forward to purchase it. In the crazy unforeseeable event (full-on sarcasm here), someone decides that the product is not for them, be okay with it. They've seen your product enough to know what it is, what it does and should someone else pop up with a need, your brand may be the first to come to mind as a word of mouth referral. Focus on your ideal customer.

Place effort and time into education marketing and how to know when to leave well enough alone.
Great points, but my marketing still isn't working, and I can't figure it out. If the person you truly consider your customer isn't drawn to your marketing, therefore not pressing the "learn more" or "buy" button. There's another culprit. What I've found was certain words, phrasing simply wasn't resonating. I was talking to the right person, yet my marketing efforts (ads, posts, emails - well, not my emails (they were bomb) were telling them this product wasn't a good fit to meet their needs. And so I had to flashback into my eczema mom brain, listen to their complaints and exact wording. Then I had to begin to use what they deem as important for my marketing.

In the eczema world, there are two main trains of thought, the traditional route of steroid creams, all things topical and internal, prescribed by the doctor. Over time eczema will disappear with age, or you'll use a series of medications until it passes or to control it over the years to come. There's the other route, the opposite end of the spectrum, where some things on the inside of us are triggering eczema. Something about their environment or their gut causing eczema symptoms to surface. How can we isolate these triggers, pinpoint the culprit, then remove any trace of eczema? No matter which path, a problematic side effect of eczema is itching, leading to continuous scratching.

Pause.

I have enough information gathered from listening to my audience, hopping inside their day to day life with eczema, even looking at the typical journeys parents may take to solve eczema. I meet them where they are, and begin speaking to them (marketing to them).

Our product bridges the gap between the intense, crazy scratching that's keeping you up at night.
It's making you go insane. So here is the ScratchMeNot. Now that I have your attention, here are some other things to help with the scratching from our brand's perspective, a holistic standpoint, from the inside out.

Its here I can begin to teach or help them need beyond the surface scratching. We've addressed what's most important to the customer, scratching. The customers aren't as concerned about anything else I have to say or sell them until their most pressing pain point is taken care of.

Introducing, the importance of a value ladder or funnels to guide your customers to their next steps without them has to search for it themselves.

And remember their main pain point is what I'm most concerned about product-wise. What is it for your products or brand? Biggest pain point, most excited about? What emotion they're trying to re-create again and again. All products aren't solving a problem per se. Take mermaid blankets, they don't necessarily help a true problem but more of a fun luxury item. In these cases, hone in on what's most important to your customer, market to them accordingly to where it resonates with them.

If you made your product because of your own problem, map out where you were before during and after the problem was solved permanently. Or is it ever solved for good? If not, focus on the repetitive cycle - on average, how many times do they go through this? It could be an opportunity for a subscription plan.

Look at your list of customers for the past month, does what you see make sense now? While most will match your demographics alone, they all align with the pain point journey.
Understand the journey that they're going through, different pain points, milestones, and experiences in all of your marketing and in your community. Speak to that. By doing this, you will never run out of content. And they'll never get tired of telling you how to sell more products to them.

Picture a company selling 1 ply toilet paper. If you're marketing it to a mom who's one place of solitude is being alone in the bathroom, she has no desire to even think of buying 1 ply toilet paper.

This is her one place of stereotypical peace, but us moms in the trenches know little ones (BIG and small) around the world hear bathroom doors click from a mile away and run towards it while formulating questions as they get closer to the threshold.

The bathroom is her one place of being alone for a quick breather. She's also buying toilet paper that can stand the test of tiny butts she has to chase down day and night. She doesn't want to forsake her fingers for a mess at any time. It must not fail. One-ply toilet paper doesn't apply to her. It may be time to switch applications or ideal customers. Now as much as this mom loves her luxury experience, she understands she simply cannot use 3-ply for the camping experience. Personally, I had no idea why 1 ply tissue existed until I went camping. She wants to be reassured this 1ply tissue will break down, in the pop up's sewage system.

Or market to the mom who loves to go on nature / hiking trips and needs light 1ply tissue on the go for the go. How can I market to her to show we are THE go-to source when it's time for hiking or camping? Answer this million-dollar question, and you'll see an uptick in checkouts.

Now here's another option. And this may or may not work. It depends on how good you are with marketing. I remember a story of someone who loved this certain toilet paper brand, but her husband went shopping for the family and bought the cheap one-ply tissue, and she was not having it. Very upset, she missing that quilted luxury fluffy feeling she asked herself what do I do with all this tissue. *Ping* *lightbulb* When family comes over, we'll use it for them. It'll ensure a short stay. Ha! She saved the good stuff for herself & her family. Use this economy tissue for the others. Can you imagine the fun you could have with that commercial? I'm joking. Or am I? Match your product to your customer demographics plus timeline. Decide on your brand's tone. One, engaging with your audience to understand what they think they need even though you know what they need. Two, position the brand as THE solution. Three, Focus on getting the best ROI for whatever marketing you're putting out there. Four, stay relevant. Evolve. See how the market is shifting; adjust with it by standing out.

What worked two years ago may not work today. The same goes for your audience. When I first began, ScratchMeNot, many moms had a hunch food & the environment triggered Eczema, but the doctors and the internet were not confirming their suspensions. Lots of room for education as the Internet has aged, so has the information. Now there's loads of information about the connections between eczema and food. Even doctors are confirming our eczema mom's original intuition. Anyone can now simply Google hundreds of thousands of different tips and remedies to try for Eczema and whether you want to go to a holistic or traditional. And everything in between.

The problem my customers are battling today is the crazy amount of info overload AND conflicting data. Yet the same underlying problems for my products remain the same.

If I ever became complacent, stopped engaging with my audience, I'd lose the pulse on these shifts. I'd notice a downtick in marketing efforts that use to lead to sales.

This is the non-sexy part of entrepreneurship. Many want to bypass this uber important step and go straight to selling because they feel like "I know my customer so well." I'm going to go just put this out there and sell it. And then a couple of months later, three months later, six months later, when they're sales are still trickling in little by little when they should be miles away from where they started.

A company that drives this point home is Smile Dentistry. Dentistry market often uses an antiquated marketing model. Commercials always show some braces, lots of bright light pictures of smiling, happy families, smiles and teeth, and a dentist wearing a white coat or blue scrubs. Years of very sterile, no true personality marketing. Just come get your teeth cleaned or dentures. Get some braces for your kids. When Smile dentistry came along, they knew exactly who they were targeting young millennials who want the Hollywood or reality TV smile. Smile's angle was and is to make dentistry sexy.

We want to make getting your teeth cleaned, whitened, or whatever you need to get done a sexy thing. Tapping into the vanity metrics blowing all dentistry marketing away. Looking at the visuals itself, they were fresh, lively, and attention-grabbing dark photos focusing strictly on how fabulous this male or female was. They even changed the dentist character from a father-like figure to a cutting fashion edge professional who happened to be a dentist. So they made the whole campaign to be this thing of getting your sexy back. Channeling Justin Timberlake as the inspiration or the heart of this campaign.

Take it a step further, a pain point for many people when it comes to dentists, they are afraid. They think of pain, aren't sure what to expect, and in return, they avoid the dentist's office or go only focusing on the fear / pain. Smile's focus isn't on the work; instead, they lean on the end result. Do you want to look and feel sexy? And the best way to do that is through your smile. and not only that, they were campaigns where they were giving y away free teeth whitening and lipstick because they understood that people's confidence is centered around their smile . Why lipstick? If you get the right shade, it makes your teeth look whiter and brighter with or without whitening.

Notice, their marketing wasn't around creating a pain-free stress-free environment. They can't promise that. But what they can promise is when you get these veneers, braces, teeth whitening, add some lipstick to that, you will be sexy. For this demographic specifically, that's the solution they want.

How do we know that the campaign is working is? They're constantly opening up new branches. Dentistry is definitely saturated. Proving if you have the right angle, plan, and budget, you're able to nab some of that very over-saturated market everyone swore you couldn't tap into.
Every corner of a metroplex seems to have another dentist's office, whether it's targeting kids or adults. I'm sure the Mint Dentistry marketing team's conversation went something like this. "How are we going to stand out? Is it going to be another billboard with the guy in a white lab coat, and I'm holding the dental pick with the child sitting in the chair? Or is it going to be, having a guy who looks nothing like the typical dentist focusing on how great our eye-catching customer is going to look when they're done?"

Oversaturation is a myth. It's easy for people to buy into. It's an easy answer. "Oh, my products didn't sell because of the market. I had too many competitors, not enough customers. Okay, cool. What key elements did you really fail at? What key elements could you really work on? Was it the fact that you weren't selling your product in multiple ways? Were you speaking to your ideal customers? Was it the fact that your niche was too broad? If you're in a heavily competitive market figure out what niche is available, how can you tap into it how much the market is available for that niche? Or was it the fact that your product pricing was not conducive to what you were selling.

Walking into this pool of competitive sharks requires a brand to shake up the market and/or have a big marketing / ads budget. Or to tap into a portion of the niche that was being ignored or undersold to.

Before emails start popping into my inbox saying you disagree, I do want to preface this with research. If your research shows a small audience of 50,000 people worldwide, your sales are going to be tapped at some point unless product diversification enters the picture.

Smile Dentistry had heavy radio and billboard ads in rotation, alongside strong branding. Something other franchises weren't doing. How will you shake up or tap into sales for your products?

When going against the grain or joining any market, opposition may arise both internally or externally. This is also why you must stay in tune with your audience and turn them into customers. Turn your audience into buyers and your buyers into raving, repeat customers.

CONVERSATIONS CREATE CONVERSIONS

While you may not have Shark Tank's show or a heavy ads budget to help speed up the process, you do have the art of conversation. Everyone has this superpower. It's just a matter of tapping into it. Remember, the more conversations you have, the more sales conversions just think about how drop shippers create sales. They start conversations. They don't look like the typical social media posts. They create "wow" buy me posts or moments. They shine a spotlight unforgettable or scroll stopping products. They position them in front of people they can sell to again and again. These types of posts get people to engage by liking, commenting, or following whatever call to action the seller wants the buyer to take.

Conversation is the natural step before conversions.

You may have heard of Steve Harvey's book, Act like a woman, think like a man. The whole premise was showing women how to navigate through the dating seasons through a man's perspective without losing their touch as a woman. It was a playbook to figuring out if a man was truly into you for real OR if he's just taking up unnecessary space in your life.

It requires a woman to slow down to see the signs the guy is giving, so she's able to decide to stay or move on quickly. Sometimes people need a playbook, even for getting the relationships they desire.

I'm challenging you to Act like a customer, Think like a business. Take off your business hat and put on your customer hat to sell more through a continual conversation with your community.

MAKE CONVERSIONS HAPPEN ON PURPOSE

Community is only one part of my Three Point Focus - this eCom trifecta is comprised of 3 points - Community, Conversions, and Collaborations. They feed each other, ultimately keeping your business healthy, sales diverse, and customers on the edge of their seats waiting to buy more based on the connection they have to your brand. Your store's conversions occur on your website, Point number two, is the primary way to make sales without directly selling to anyone. It's the place you can receive the most profit and sleep sales.

The website is a simple and yet sometimes tricky beast. There is a movie called Field of Dreams I haven't even seen it yet. I hear one of its famous quotes over and over again saying. "If you build it, they will come." And many sellers believe this myth that if you build it, they will come. And so off, they go creating websites that look amazing yet have little to no traffic and even worse have no conversion. So there stuck thinking what's wrong with me? What's wrong with my products?

Why don't they want to buy my product?

Why aren't they coming to my store online?

When jumpstarting a business, you have to have your own place for sales.

What many don't tell you is that you have to constantly and consistently drive traffic to your store online on your website. So let's focus on the numbers for a moment. If 100 people come to your website, if you have your site set up as an average store, about three of them will purchase, giving us a 3% conversion rate. Considering we are catching people at different points in their buying process, this statistic makes sense. If you've taken into consideration the community I've outlined previously, these numbers could reach beyond 20%.

Either way, all 100 won't buy today. So if you leave with 3 buyers, you're on target.

Now outside of the community that you've built, let's say, in a Facebook group where you have two hundred people in it. You should be having several conversations on various topics within their pain points or just life in general and positioning your product for sale. Outside of this space, we want to make sure that we're leaving some breadcrumbs leading people to our website to get acclimated to our brand and eventually buy.

The marketing industry says it takes about seven times for a person to come in contact with your brand before they are ready to make a purchase. With the Internet in place, it has decreased our attention span drastically. Now experts are saying it takes 21 times of brand exposure before making a buying decision. Therefore not only do we need to expose our brand also need to give them good, solid reasons to come to our website by having different marketing efforts in place. Facebook ads, Facebook group, Instagram, emails, YouTube, blogs, google ads, and the list goes on and on.

If a person is new to our brand, we have marketing catered to turning newbies into customers. If a person is an existing customer, we market to turn them into a repeat customer. If a repeat customer, we want to turn them into a raving, referring fan.
We're going to go through a few of the key elements that make a website work in our favor and highlight what doesn't work.

If you haven't noticed by now, the whole point of a website is to sell something. Plain and simple. Our store visitors think they are hopping on your website to look around, learn, and buy. However, unbeknownst to them, we are guiding their path; they think they're navigating through our store willingly.

From today forward, when you think about your online store, think about this funnel or flow:

- Drive traffic / people to our website
- Sign up for our mailing list to get a discount or free gift
- Highlighting a product or collection
- If / then add to cart options, otherwise known as up or down sells
- Checkout with particular cart value in mind

An ad caught my eye; it was a hair care line for women of color with an array of curly textured hair. It hit a couple of pain points that women of color go through right from the start. One of our gripes is we spend a lot of money for a small amount of hair product, yet our hair requires a lot of hair product. Usually, it doesn't last long. This company said you know what, let's put three products in one. And on top of that, let's make the jars three times bigger than everyone else. And so they created a product they say works amazingly great. They have a lot of social proof, testimonials, and videos which is required in this industry. (Another hidden barrier to purchase, for hair care, we don't buy unless we can see the before and after with our type of hair). Their website was as ugly as can be but effective. They simply had one product.

What made this company stand out was how they marketed it to women tired of a closet full of hair products, running out of one but not the other or running out too soon because our hair requires massive amounts of product. Number one - its three products in one, saving crazy time and energy in application and hair fuss. Number two, it is larger than all other competitors, and it is saving you money based on looks alone. No more barrier to purchase - the container of product is huge. Number three, I'm saving money. I don't have to buy several bottles of different products to make this 3 in 1 product.

On top of this, they placed this product on their website with massive amounts of social proof, & testimonials, yet about the products themselves Even though they had one product available, there were three options for purchase.

Here's where the fun begins. Three options, good, better, and best in a non-sequential order. Good, best, and better. Drawing your eye to Best with have seals of approval and the best money-saving deal. Now with one product, you might be wondering, well, what is good, better, and best? Here we go, cue the three little bears. Good - the price for one bottle is the most expensive. Better is middle ground savings selling two. The best deal per bottle selling three was the best option.

Visually with seals of approval, deals, and making the best option larger than the others you now, you're getting three of the same thing. Therefore, you've increased your shopping cart value by feeding into one of the original qualms with curly-haired women. We hate running out of a good thing. The thoughts we're projecting: Why run out? You know you're going to love it. Look at all the testimonials and social proof. Why buy just one when you can save and buy three.
To take the marketing cake, they are also providing you with >>> free shipping. The Amazon way is Amazon prime free shipping. And thanks to Amazon, online shoppers have grown accustomed to free shipping that Amazon is willing to actually losing money by offering this because they know their numbers. Once a person becomes an

Amazon customer, they're likely to get addicted to shopping with us. Thus making them more money.

Taking a lesson straight out of Amazon's playbook, let's take a closer look.

Amazon's whole mission in life is to be the only source for whatever you need to buy. They will figure out a way to upsell, cross-sell, sell a customer more, and make that money back in different ways. One of the key ways being through memberships. Amazon makes more money in their memberships than they do selling all of their products combined.

I didn't buy the hair product mentioned. But I imagine if I purchased 3 bottles of their product, I wouldn't have a need to go back to purchase for a while. They'd need to find a way to keep me buying from them, even if I didn't need the product right now.

A subscription would be the next step.

How can you position your product, sell it the same way? Your website gives you plenty of flexibility and the opportunity to sell the same product in several different ways.

Could it be a quick product bundle or setting up a subscription??

Is there a way that you can increase your cart value simply by giving your customers an opportunity to buy more of it, inserting a bit of scarcity and adding a discount or free shipping?

What can you do to increase sales? Now, this is such an amazing opportunity because many people overlook this. They think, why would someone purchase three of these things? Why would they want to purchase five of these things? Without reason, they won't. This company decided to position the reason before the question was even asked.

How?

Storytelling marketing with pain points, FAQ's, and social proof. Present your products as the solution to the problem you've highlights starts an internal and external conversation. Before they even think about opposing questions or objections, you're answering them before their eyes, increasing the conversion rate. Now, you're optimizing your site, and you're making sure that they don't have to go search around for answers. They're staying focused inside your funnel without leaving prematurely. Distractions avoided. With a designated step by step path for your customers in place, we can talk more on conversion rates we touched on earlier. Calculate the number of sales you had each day, week, month, and year and divide that by the number of visitors for the same amount of time. And this is your conversion rate. Now, one of the best ways to increase your conversion rate is to drive the right traffic to your website.

Check.

Community in place.

Another way to increase your conversion rate is to optimize your website through funnel flow and SEO. There's always room to continue optimizing. I remember talking to the owner of City Kitty, Rebecca Rescate, as she was in the process of changing her website, adding more information to it, making it more up to date, and aesthetically pleasing. After all, the website had an infomercial vibe to it, primary colors, lots of "as seen in" stamps, the works. She had just got off the phone with her web designer, who made all the changes requested. It looked magnificent, but she was not happy because the conversion rate plummeted. She said, "I don't know where we went wrong but put it back the way that it was because conversion rates are more important than a pretty website." (paraphrased) Out of the mouth of the multi-million dollar, brand comes straight #truth. I bet if you go to their website now, it's still the original site. The same thing goes for you. Sometimes we get so caught up on having a pretty website that we don't understand the power of converting visitors into customers. Your website is business. Nothing personal. Its' sole purpose is to catch their attention, educate them, and position your products for sale.

To encourage the sale, have these key things in place.

1) Pictures of happy faces (or pets) the end emotion the customer wants themselves. (Before and after pics come in handy, think of weight loss products)
2) Simple education or learning moments, easy to understand why this product is needed. (Product descriptions, FAQs, storytell your way through the journey).
3) Ways to encourage your customers to purchase more cross-sells (priced similar to the primary product), upsells (higher priced), and down sells (lower price). Don't worry if only a few purchases initially, you're going to be testing to see what works and what doesn't work.
4) And an easy checkout process.

No one wants to click 90 times just to check out. Amazon does the one-click checkout. Why? No-fuss checkouts mean you don't have to fumble around for your wallet or for your purse to look for your credit card information. Hence why PayPal and Amazon both make it easy for you to save your credit card & any other information on file. Ease of checkout. And that's why the one-click checkout works so fluidly. The same thing when it came to the Crayon Case, the Crayon Case wanted to do $1 million in sales for Black Friday Weekend. They nailed this goal within 90 minutes of making their Black Friday sale live. They were hoping to accomplish it over the weekend. To reach that goal, let's reverse engineer how they were able to do this.

In order to create $1 million in sales that weekend, they prepared their customers in advance.

1. Made sure that they had $1 million in inventory in stock
2. Build up the anticipation of the BIG sale.
3. A website in place that hopefully wouldn't crash with higher than normal traffic But here's the thing that they did for their customers days leading to the sale
4. Prepare their customers for the sale.

If you scroll through their social media, they are telling their customers exactly what to do to ensure they get the big sale items they really want.

They're telling them, hey,

1. Go into your account if you don't have one, create an account,
2. 12dd your products that you want to purchase to your cart now because as soon as the sale comes, we cannot guarantee that the products will actually be in stock the long enough for you to purchase.
3. So prepare in advance if you have credit card information, add that to the account so that it's easier for you to check out. Because when we turn on the sale, when we make sure, you don't miss out.

Whew, strategy on ten!

Okay. So what just happened here? The Crayon Case started with the end in mind, as my husband always says. One, they prepared their customers in advance, had them thinking about their wish list in advance, what they wanted to purchase e once it went on sale. They also said here's what's not going to be on sale, avoiding any confusion and disappointment. Clarity is key. It inserts a bit of scarcity. There's only a limited amount, and once it's gone, it's gone. And it's going to take us some time before we restock. A smart move on their behalf, there were a few products their customers were clamoring for. Instead of adding it back to stock as soon they were available, they dropped it for sale. Another level of scarcity and exclusivity as they made this public knowledge to social media followers, email subscribers, and even on their website.

And then here's the other thing that they did, which I think they did remarkably well. They kept reminding their fans of the sale and steps required to be the first to snag their wish list items with influencers constantly flooding their social pages reminding fans of the creative possibilities, proof the products are being used by the best make-up artists available, testimonials and proof of others using Crayon Case products

While their customers were not aware of their internal goal, staff within the Crayon Case's staff were all on board to help reach this goal. By training their visitors and customers to take the next step towards the checkout sale, completing the conversion from visitor to a sale.

While this was an awesome way to prepare its customers, it also gave the company an opportunity to have an estimate sales based on wish lists & cart values. Now they are able to see the effects of the marketing, then determine what shifts need to be made.
This is why it is so important for us to become a student of our customers and our business. There are strategic elements we can put in place to expedite our success and move to our sales that much faster. Now, the fun part about conversion rates is that every time you make a sale you are also widening and increasing your footprint for your movement. So never forget to instill your story into the process still. I

think over the years, even myself, I have gotten so focused on making sure little ones get their ScratchMeNots, and all the moving pieces of the puzzle are in place, I sometimes even forget - constantly retell our story.

The Crayon Case keeps its continuing story in focus. As soon as they hit $1M in sales, the owner Supa Cent posted a video on her social pages showing her reaction. This alone made her fans go crazy with excitement that their sales were a contributing factor to their success. Can you imagine that? Customers were excited their order helped the company reach their first $1M in a day? Their Know, Like, Trust factor grew, causing more fans to rave over them.

When Sephora came out with a knock off version of the Crayon Cases' brand & products, it was the fans who rang the alarm. Coming to their defense and letting others know of how a big brand was trying to snuff out the light of a smaller company.

The Crayon Case achieved something many brands are dreaming of. Brand loyalty. The power of an engaged community with products available for sale on your website turns into a symbiotic relationship where one feeds the other. One cannot thrive without the other.

On average, 20% of your existing customers create 80% of your sales and revenue.

You better believe the Crayon Case and all other companies mentioned are creating conversions through email with their existing customers. The better we nurture our email list, the better chances we have of the stabilizing our business by selling more. Our raving fans are not going to come from those who have never used our product before. They're those who love our products, can't say enough of it, and use it on a consistent or repetitive basis.

There's an art to social media. And before you start thinking it, Email marketing is not dead, as many are trying to say. It is alive and kicking. It's a powerful way to convert a conversation into a sale.

EMAIL THEM. THEY'LL PAY YOU FOR IT

Let's slow down to speed up. When we look at, our email list, instead of just seeing subscribers or visitors see them as people. And when you introduce, when you request from one to be a subscriber to your list, you introduce them to you for the first time via email — First Impressions matter. Thanks to social media, we as a whole have shorter attention spans. Now With the 21 times, it takes to expose a brand online to a customer, those same people are constantly being interrupted by the internet, social media, and the constant need to know "what's next." If it's not grabbing our attention, we are simply moving on to something else.

As a business, the only thing that is consistent is change. There's nothing we can do about that except evolve. And so with email marketing, this is a perfect opportunity to connect with new subscribers. Turn them from a visitor to customer and then apply the 80/20 rule to turn them into raving repeat customers.

Here's the fun part about email marketing; we are able to do this through something called email sequences Communications that allow us to take our subscribers on a specific journey. This journey has many calls to actions (CTAs) where we're going to request or ask them to do certain things. Maybe it's to reply to an email, maybe it's purchasing a product, joining our community, and in the example of the Crayon Case, it was to follow these Black Friday Sale instructions. Each email has an opportunity to present different actions for them to take. Now, these emails are a part of the ultimate goal to create a lasting impression on our customers. Give them valuable content and great products to purchase again and again.

With email marketing, there's a process to actually taking a person from just a reader to now an action taker to ultimately a buyer. And so we're going to dissect this.

As soon as someone becomes a subscriber, we get a short window of opportunity to keep their attention and have them open, click, and want to learn more about us. They're already interested because they have either subscribed to our list or purchase a product that added them to our list, which we then foster that relationship.

Most likely, your emails have ended in a vast sea of other emails, so it must stand out with a subject line, the "from name" has to be recognizable or unique. It's gotta have a call to action to get you out of the promotions section. For example, "Reply and tell me what you think of…"

Once your email has been opened, let the games begin (in my "Hunger Games" voice).

I love to use Russell Brunson's soap opera method, which is where we're going to take them on a high energy, high drama journey through.

Five emails. You can make it longer, you can make it shorter, but five gives you a good way to break up a story, a small story. It could be of your storyline of how you came into existence. Not literally, just your products or brand). Whatever it is, it must keep their attention and make them anxious to read the next email.

Having conversations with customers through email gives plenty of opportunities to ask for the first or next sale. After you've indoctrinated them via email, you'll typically talk about 1 -3 topics, mixing in stories, tips, quotes, controversy, and information setting you and your brand as the Go-To source. Pro tip- Turn these emails into blog posts, social media posts to harness the power of search engine optimization, getting new eyes on your store and products organically.

While my email marketing tool suggestions in my Little Black Book for e-commerce, here are a few pointers.

1. It's reasonably priced. Notice I didn't recommend free. We want our emails to be seen and, if possible, skip the promotions box or label. Research has shown, email provides with free accounts attract spammers. Google and others filter their email according to the email marketing tool. Those with paid accounts have a higher likelihood of emails being read by the subscriber due to Google's sorting.
2. No matter which tool you use, you are able to segment your list. We treat our subscribers differently depending on what type of subscriber they are. If you have a new person who's visited your website but has never made a purchase, our emails will be focused on loving them towards the sale.

If we have a first time customer, we want them to tell us what they think of their purchase and buy again. Different pathways depending on the type of subscriber. You could imagine how awkward it would be to send a repeat customer a "here's a coupon off your first order" email, instead of "Here's $10 off your next order for being a VIP."

Being able to segment or tag your list is key because you want to see what your subscribers and customers are doing with your emails. Are they reading them? Did they click on that Buy link?, You want to be able to move people within your email container based on actions, interests, based on how they are engaging with your content.

3. We want to know how many emails or actions are they actually doing. Scoring is amazing. it lets you know who was taking action, who is inactive, who is weighing down your list, and then when it's time to do your quarterly or annual cleanse of your email list, you now know exactly who to pay attention to and who to let go of.

4. 4. Are you actually making money from your emails? And if you send an email today, how quickly will you make money from that same email? Emails are designed to make you money. So if your emails are not doing their job, the problems usually lie within your content, your list, or the call to actions (CTA) within your emails. (CTA - are you clearly telling your subscribers what to do to make a purchase?)

5. Send emails automatically. Syncing your store to your email marketing tool allows you to send emails based on your visitor or customer actions on your website. Whether they are subscribing to your newsletter or purchasing a holiday bundle. When someone abandons their cart without purchasing, emails should fire, reminding them to finish their orders. Sending emails based on their actions is key to keep you top of mind as the company to fill their needs and first to mind when it's time to buy.

6. Direct your subscribers to other containers you give value, like Facebook groups or your Instagram or even for Twitter parties. It is a peek inside, of what your subscribers are doing, giving us more ways to talk to them and learn from them.

7. Are you getting your money's worth? Every single month, we are paying this email marketing tool based on how many subscribers you have, let's say a list of 10,000 people, and you have a 5% open rate, there's some dead weight. There are

inactive subscribers on your list who are no longer care about your emails, and they've either moved on, they didn't find value in your emails, or they never received them. Beyond vanity numbers, if you've tried to revive your list and emails are still remaining unopened, it's time to purge. A small engaged list will show you what's really happening with your subscribers for opens, clicks, and orders.

Email lists are not cheap, paying $50 to $500 a month depending on the vendor and size, why pay for subscribers who aren't engaging with us?

Once a quarter, once or twice a year, once a year, whatever you decide to take the time to clean up your list by making active subscribers, inactive, or delete them altogether. 8. My last and final point - Be consistent. We set up email sequences, so we don't have to consistently write an email each day. Create a schedule you can stick to, allowing your subscribers to anticipate the next email. Is it too late to begin now or fix what you have in place? Never. Everyone is stronger in one area over the other. Just begin with 5 emails and build from there. We want to talk to our customers enough to where when holidays or special events come around, and we ask for the sale, they have their credit cards ready to buy.

When you decide to create a holiday campaign, it'll be saved in your email marketing tool to reuse & edit the next year again. That's an easy way to help fill up next year's email content calendar buy using content from each month of this year.

WHEN IS ENOUGH, ENOUGH

I was talking to a fellow mom of five (yes, many of us exist ha!) who said something that stopped me in mid-sentence. She said, when do we have enough?

Some say never, others say when a particular number of sales have been hit, others say after so many lives have been touched. I almost started to feel guilty about wanting to rule the world of e-commerce and rack in hundreds of thousands, if not millions in sales each month. I have an innate competition with myself and spurring other women to be a part of the top 1% of e-commerce sales.

One day, I was listening to a sermon talking about a couple who wanted to tithe by giving beyond 10% of their income. He and his wife challenged themselves to give so much that they'd only live off 10% of their earnings, giving the other 90% away.

As I pondered on these seemingly very different perspectives, it hit me. My product came about to change lives. Matter of fact, many products were created with this same intent. I simply can't change lives if it's sitting on the shelves. And I can only touch so many lives if I sell a limited quantity.

Therefore, I have to decide how far I want my ripple to go. When we throw a pebble into the water, it leaves ripples behind, outlining where the pebble was dropped. Even though the pebble only touched a small area of water, the effects of its presence were seen far beyond its' footprint.

When growing our business, those two views on growth are really one and the same. We decide our products ripple effect by selling at our own pace.

CATCH THIS SNEAKY LITTLE LIE

A sneaky little lie can surface in an "I'm too busy raising a young family; therefore, I can't quite possibly make this a successful growing business. I'll think I'll stick to hobby level, and bring in a couple of extra dollars so I can buy the kids some new shoes, get a new bag or things of that nature. Take care of some things around the house, maybe a bill or two." I call that a lie.

One because you're reading this book, so there's something about you that wants your business to thrive and do more than help the family.

Two, just like with anything, what we place as a priority becomes something we nurture to grow. It's a sneaky lie feeling very, very real, especially if the time and energy put towards your business don't equate to substantial profit

To honor the season we are in, we move at our own pace. I remember forcing and pushing my business forward when I had two small kids. I had goals I wanted to achieve, and I was determined to surpass my goals.

I was visiting my friend, Wynter Pitts, to straighten my hair. We were talking about kids and business. I was ravenously using all my extra time and energy to grow ScratchMeNot. I looked over my shoulder, and she was like the Tortoise, from the Tortoise and the Hare story, slowly building her brand, For Girls like You, brick by brick. She was in no rush to grow; her only focus was to first help her four young girls with positive self-image messages and what God thinks of them, then reach other tweens who needed the same outlet.

She was definitely more calculated with her time, and I wanted to know why. As a mom of four, I knew her life was busy. Yet, I also knew we make time for what we want to grow. I began to ask her, why aren't you working non-stop like me? I see how big this can be. I know you do too. Why aren't your speeding towards it?

She ever so nonchalantly said, "Andrea, right now, God is showing me I need to pour myself into my girls. Family is the most important, and the business will be what it will be at the right time." In short, she continued to tell me God will order her steps, open doors for her as she honors her season.

I watched both of our businesses flourish. I saw her go on to make more magazines for tweens, write book series after series for kids and adults, co-write books with her oldest daughter and her husband, become a traveling speaker. I was honestly in awe.

Every time we talked, she had another book come out, her fan base was growing. More importantly, she stayed true to her original intent, her girls, and her family.

Then a few years after my "why" drilling, she suddenly passed away. I keep hearing her words of honoring the season we're in. In those 5ish years after our chat, she ran entrepreneurial laps moving at the same speed she always did, calculated with her family first.

She didn't forsake her family for her business.

Now don't get me wrong, I'm sure behind the scenes, there were times specifically carved out for work, deadlines to meet, overwhelming moments, goals to hit and money to make, yet she was present for her family.

My first point is to honor the season you're in.

Later I learned she too was frustrated that the career / business side of her brain wasn't being tapped into while she was in her momming season. Yet she stayed true to her course. When her oldest daughter started to hit the tweens stage, she realized there was a gap in magazines for tweens. At that moment, her purpose for her next season was revealed, and she moved into it knowing her girls were her original ministry.

There's a chapter of the Bible Ecclesiastes 3that says for everything, there is a season and a time for every matter under heaven. It then goes on to a time for this and a time for that.

Wynter's life reflected this when it came to entrepreneurship and life.

Even though it seems like everyone is running in the rat race, we don't have to subscribe to that process.

My second point is to weigh your "why."

Your business may not hit the ground running at $1M in sales the first year, then again, maybe, just maybe the goal isn't the amount revenue made. Maybe it's the number of lives we change along the way that's our true end game.

This is what keeps me going when the kids are being extra, loopy, and all-out crazy. When the house is rarely model home ready, and we have to shove clothes into a closet or empty chair when guests stop by unexpectedly or when I've ordered take-out for the 3rd time in the same week.

Perhaps your husband is confused as to why you're pursuing your own business when he makes more than enough for you to be a 100% stay at home mom.

Maybe, it's looking kind of tempting to sell the business or scale back to maintaining but not actively growing it.

There was a time I got so frustrated working so hard, yet the business won't cooperate. It wasn't until I saw other businesses succeeding, doing way less that it clicked for me. I don't have to almost kill myself to sell more products and be present for my family.

I took a survey of the fruits of my labor to see what I've done right. My children know that when they talk to me, I listen, and when they have a request, I respond. My husband knows when he comes home, there is something to eat, either I've cooked it, or ordered take out. My work time is my work time. My kids see me working, and that's okay. There are some resolves that I had to come to myself and say, "You know what? My normal isn't someone else's normal. My balance isn't someone else in the balance. I want my kids to see that there was another way to live this life."

Yes, you can go down this traditional route, school, degree, great job, climb the ladder, and succeed. You can go to school, you can thrive, and you can truly create the career that you want. But there's also another route. A road less frequently seen. Becoming an entrepreneur making your own money, skipping the corporate ladder, and going straight to being the CEO of your own corporation.

I'm paving the way for my kids to choose which route they want to take.

And yes, there's going to be some lumps and bumps along the way. There's going to be some sleepless nights. There's going to be some sacrifice. There's going to be some moments when I have to work while baby wearing or during naps (or movie time). I'm not going to deny that or paint a pretty picture.

Your business is a beautiful mirror of yourself, of your family, of your kids, and of your spouse - your life. So unlike corporate America, where we have to, or we feel like we have to, compartmentalize our lives by having a solid chunk of time and place to work away from family. And then you leave work, and you come home to your family, and then you have to squeeze in family life, homework, dinner, put the kids to bed and then you have husband time - possibly yourself. We're actually working against the grain by living a life where I happen to work to. Your own business affords you the opportunity to make one homogenous life where business work, family, kids, spouse, you are all together. The degree to which you choose.

But here's the thing, just like your children weren't born at age seven, they were newborns, and you got a chance to ease into this family lifestyle. The same thing with the business. Everyone has a starting point and learning that you don't necessarily have to have it all figured out, and it's going to ebb and flow. Breathe and know this is a living, breathing entity.

They're going to see me building a business. I want them to see some of the greatest moments created, and some of the hardest moments.

I'm not exempt. I ask myself daily, does this edify entrepreneurial life for my family, is it edifying , building , or creating that end result that I'm looking for. I challenge you to ask yourself that same questions. What is your end result that you're trying to create? What is your pace? What season are you in?

What fills your bucket to keep going as you're growing? That doesn't mean that it won't evolve. Initially, we all start with something in mind that we're trying to achieve. If you can verbalize it, write it down. Share it with your family so they can get on board, or at least see why you're tied to your computer at designated times. It becomes tangible to them too. I remember what it was like when I shipped products overseas for the first time. I remember my husband counting all the different countries our product has been sold in. Places that we have never physically been, ourselves. I was looking at countless pictures, testimonials, and quotes for moms and dads who were ever so grateful that we created this product and started to sell it. That fills my bucket that shows my kids; this is not just about money. This is not just about building a career, building a business. This is about changing someone's life, and when you can communicate that clearly to your family, they can connect with your business on a deeper level. The support and grace can flows easier towards you.

Disclaimer: Support is not a prerequisite for your success. And I had to get that through my brain. I think one of the crazy things about this entrepreneur's life is a success (whatever your definition of it is) can be achieved under the most intense circumstances. Lisa Nichols came to mind when I was kind of new to this whole mindset, manifesting, and thought process.

Her story alone hit a chord in my mind, reinforcing a concept I learned as a child - Anything is possible, limitations are for someone else. Her story began at her lowest point. She ran out of diapers for her son, and for 3 days, she had to use towels and t-shirts in lieu of pampers for him. She didn't have enough money to buy any. Ran out of checks and not enough in the bank to withdraw from an atm. Out of frustration, she told her son, who was only months old, that she would never be here again. With a closet as an office, mirrors on the wall giving illusions to make it larger than what it really was, she began to work herself out of the financial valley she found herself in as a single mom.

It took her some time. It wasn't a light switch, as soon as she said it, the next day they were living the life that she envisioned. But vividly saw and worked toward her end goal. And she did whatever it took to create that. It meant some discomfort. It meant some focus. And it also meant pushing past the naysayers, pushing past those who didn't support her, tuning them out so that she could focus on what she was trying to create. I flashed to myself, and I said, Andrea, if you ever had to be a single mom, what would you do? What would you do to build this business? Or would you shut it down, get a regular job or figure this thing out?

What is it about Lisa Nichols? She can look at her situation, almost step out of herself to say, this is not where I'm supposed to be. I'm supposed to be over there. She then hopped back into herself and began the journey to get where she is today.

What is it about me that I need to tap into so that I can have that laser beam focus to get where I need to get to the end to bring my family along with it. I don't want something catastrophic to happen to turn that on. I don't want my kids to almost graduate high school and head off to college after 15 years of being an entrepreneur before I turned it on. I want that turned on now because I want them to experience and see the journey in full circle - highs, lows, and fruits of my labor. Based on a snippet of my journey, they can decide if entrepreneurship is for them. Your "why" is one of the cornerstones guiding you through challenges of selling products present, while your strategy ensures your selling footprint will support it.

COLLABORATIONS: POSITIONING & SELLING ON SOMEONE ELSE'S PLATFORM

Over the course of the life of a business, there's a lot of decisions, guessing, and risk-taking. I even hate to admit the amount of money invested and lost, yet there was also a whole lot more made. You know the saying, if I knew what I know today, my yesterday would be so different. But so would my today. (Yeah I paraphrased). There were many times when I was so close but not on target. But I was on to something.

My first big oops was before I was even selling products. I took my design and limited fabric knowledge, went to JoAnn Fabrics, and I bought enough fabric for 300 units. My excitement came crashing down when I realized that almost every single unit made was defective. We had to redo the entire order with a new design. Apparently, fabric works a bit differently than studs and beams.

Then there was the time I was 9 months pregnant, talking on the phone with a friend. A contraction hits a harder than the usual Braxton Hicks, and I thought hmmm…that was a bit strong. I casually tell my friend I might be in labor, but remember, I need to get some orders out. I get off the phone with her to call my husband to tell him, "I think it's time," and he races home.
I'm in the middle of labor, one of the fastest deliveries on my life, and all I can think about is processing orders, closing business with clients overseas, and microwaving a sock full of rice to apply to my contractions to buy me some thinking time.

While it was a great way to distract myself from the pain, it definitely highlighted my need to hire some help. My husband walked through the door, confused, pacing from room to room, wondering if we should really leave for the hospital or stick it out. Not wanting to risk it, we left. Racing down the highway, contracts 2 minutes apart, we barely made it to the hospital. Two hours later, my son was born. But he missed it. Talk about a Lifetime movie in the making.

And yes, I got those orders out!

I could rattle off several other "business oops" that took me by storm, orders getting stuck in customs, Amazon jail, price increases, getting funding to scale at the very last minute, my list goes on and on. My point for telling you all of these blunders (or heroic labors, ha!) is to start with the end in mind.

As we make moves towards our goals, move as if we are already at the level of business we want to be at. How would the business operation without you? How would it generate sales? What can you do to automate the process?

I should have taken a friend's advice when I had my firstborn. "Andrea, stop reading parenting books, you'll go cross-eyed with contradicting information and insane from all the ways you can miss the mark in rearing your child."

And it just so happened that I started building my business right at the peak of starting my family. Lots of mom guilt poured into my head. Should I be spending this much time growing a business when I could be spending it with the kids? Should I put all of this effort into their needs? Even my husband? I battled that for a while because from what I read (and what's drilled into new mothers), the first five years are the most fundamental years of life. If we mess this up, we've essentially jacked up my children, who will then need therapy throughout their adulthood. Talk about a lot of pressure.

There's no true way to get around mom guilt, child development, our parent's perception of our parenting skills, husband's fav question "So what'd you do today" and everything in between… except to face it & tackle it head-on. How we, as sellers, do it? By protecting our time and maximizing our sales.

Sleeping Baby, a company that sells a product named Zipadee Zip, decided to stick to the model of selling its product only on their website. No wholesalers or stores could carry their line. They wanted full control (and profit) from their products. They chose a product selling model of selling direct to customer, and it worked for them.

But guess what they recently added after their Shark Tank episode explosion. Amazon.

Why? They were making crazy bank on their website, why expand?
They did something we all should consider if we want to grow within the limitations of our time. Diversify your streams of sales. Everyone wants multiple streams of revenue, but have you considered selling the same product in multiple ways to create healthy streams of income for your business.

Sleeping Baby (amazing search engine friendly, keyword filled brand name by the way) was so stuck on selling their product in one way; they almost missed out on sales they would have never tapped in without it.

Once they had a solid stream of sales on their website, they knew tapping into Amazon's customers would give them access to a new steady stream of customers who love and trust Amazon. Amazon customers are loyal. Amazon, in return, rewards its customers with free shipping, fast delivery, no-hassle returns, one-click checkout, Prime Membership...those customers go to Amazon for almost all of their needs.

Sleeping Baby made a small but lucrative pivot to adding a wholesaler, Amazon, to their list and began selling their product. With no other retailers or wholesalers selling Zipadee Zips on Amazon, they created a small monopoly for their product, causing all customers who want one, to purchase through them on America's favorite online store. This tiny shift allows Sleeping Baby to grow exponentially given proper inventory levels

If you look at your products and you're not selling them in multiple ways, it is time to decide your next stream of revenue to take your brand to the next level.

The key difference between having your own website and selling your products on a third-party collaborations like Amazon is that for your website, you are in charge and control of everything. You are also responsible to drive traffic to your website - then to your products - then to the checkout page to close the buying circuit - making the sale. We are in charge of conversion. Should your online store have key elements in place, you'll have every opportunity to connect with your visitors through email, social media, etc., to turn your customers your existing customers into repeat customers. All of this is in your control.

For Amazon, eBay, Etsy, walmart.com, or any other 3rd party selling platforms, their whole purpose of existing is to do what you would do for your own website. Drive people to their piece of the internet to see their selection of products, turn them into a customer, then turn them into a rapidly dependent customer buying again and again.

However, to do this on a larger scale, Amazon allows vendors to sell products on their platform to attract each of their ideal audience as well for sales. On the flip side of that same money-making coin, there are many restrictions, little access to how the website flows and functions, or what information we are able to capture from Amazon's customer. Which just so happens to be our customer too, but not legally.

Yet unlike our website, where we receive the most profit, 3rd party selling platforms give us instant exposure to their hundreds of thousands of buying customers for a fee. Remember earlier I mentioned Sleeping Baby added their first (only) wholesaler?

Whenever we decide to sell our products, whether to drop ship, wholesale, direct to customer, etc. we have to make sure it aligns with our selling model and if our product aligns with theirs.

I consider Amazon, a wholesaler.

Amazon is designed for massive inventory turnover & sales. It just so happens they are selling directly to the customer. However, if you take a closer look, the name of their game is high volume sales. They drive crazy traffic to their website to make the most money through their vendors, and their higher fees reflect it to gain access to Amazon's customers. Due to the possibilities of high volume sales, your price (-) your cost of goods (+) their fees (=) your profit, Amazon looks more and more like a wholesaler.

Many get very frustrated with Amazon's fees in comparison to Etsy, but they are running different selling models.

For instance, when looking at Etsy. It was originally designed for high-quality handmade products. Handmade meaning the seller has made the product by their own hand and/or by their team's hands. Etsy has since deviated from the original definition, but we won't go down that rabbit trail.

Etsy's fees are relatively low because they understand how much time and energy it takes to produce handmade products. Depending on the product, the seller cannot make hundreds of thousands of products to get crazy sales — a low listing & commission fee in exchange for access to Etsy's customers. I deem Etsy similar to the Direct to customer selling model based on the rate of inventory turnover (the rate at which inventory is selling over a select period of time).

Considering our websites do not have 100's of thousands of people on it as soon as we make our website live, it makes sense to pay for access to their customers to get a piece of the e-commerce pie.

When selling on a different channel, it's helpful to understand what makes it tick. How do you get customers to your listing, how do you get the reviews or feedback necessary to be seen organically, how do we maximize ads without overspending, what do we do to create loyal customers on someone else's site? How do we sell well when Etsy or Amazon purposefully show our competitors on our products page?

No matter where we sell our products, we must go through the same trial and error and test strategies we would do on our own website.

But selling goes beyond the obvious online store transaction, it comes with positioning our brand on someone else's channel. Earlier, we were building a community of our own, but now we're focusing on letting other communities know we exist.

Have you ever seen a product go viral? Or the Oprah effect? That's the power of positioning a brand on another's platform for sales both now and later. Or brands clamoring to get an influencer to wear their products on their YouTube channel or talk about it on their blog post.

That's positioning.

Why is this important? We can only get so far, so fast on our own. No matter how amazing your marketing or ad skills are, it takes paying for someone else's audience to surpass your goals.

Have you ever noticed when a movie is on the verge of coming out, movie stars interview on every single TV channel known to man, social media outlet, blog post, press release, and article available? Because each outlet has its own buying audience. On top of that, there's a movie premiere with all the stars the media shines a light on.

Publicity on top of publicity.

When a movie is released, it's available worldwide to every movie theatre - its sales channels.

Why?

Their #1 priority is to get butts in seats to make this movie a box office hit for opening weekend. Equaling hundreds of millions of dollars, or more considering the most expensive movie made of all time, was Pirates of the Caribbean: On Stranger Tides, it made over $1 billion worldwide.

The power of cross-promotion and anticipation for its' release is a strategy used time and time again to make it a box office hit because it works. Pulls all audiences toward the same Big event at the same — genius and duplicatable.

The same with your brand. It's one thing to make the product; it's another thing to sell it with ease. Cross-promotion for many sellers means ads; the easiest way to be consistent and constant reach new audiences. Outside of my fav 3rd party platform being Amazon, collaborations go beyond selling on someone else's website. Remember, Sleeping Baby had what some would say were impressive sales before the owners went on Shark Tank.

But it was getting their brand on the show in front of millions where they were able to reach the next level of sales.

Again, you may not have access to a TV show like Shark Tank's audience today, but you can start to connect with other's audiences, both big and small. I'll sprint through a list of possibilities with high impact:

Social Media: Swaps, postings, guest appearances
Guest blog posts and magazine articles, influencers, Podcast interviews, Local & National TV Appearances, whatever you choose, be consistent.

More than pitching to be seen, form relationships both parties can benefit from for years to come. We're not shooting for a hit and run; we're looking to fill a void within their community. Whether it's information or through our product directly, then we'll be asked back to share again, thus positioning your products and brand as the "Go-To" product or even you, being the subject matter expert.

The Oprah Effect can happen for anyone through relationships, creative pitching angles, understanding "no" is part of the process, and consistency. Creating your own ripple effect.

Consistency is the glue holding my 3 point focus - Community, Conversions, and Collaborations together.

BUT WHAT ABOUT THE MONEY

It would be a big disservice to us both if I were to set you up for success as to how to sell your products faster, but didn't talk about our money flow and goals. More importantly, how to make money serve us.

Our greatest asset is our list of subscribers & buying customers. Depending on where you are in business, you need to focus on one of two things now money or long-term money. (
If your store is in need of traffic and sales, you must focus on NOW money. This is the money that is going to breathe life into the store, keep the lights on, and buys you time to reach your next financial goal. To gain NOW money, get in front of customers in person to make sales now and online consistently, and drive traffic to your website. Unless you have an engaged community in place or a marketing budget for ads, online is going to be a slower path to the dollar bills. Technically, online sales require a ramp-up as it's a path passive sales.

Yes, all the FB lives are building opportunities for sales, but today they may not provide large consistent sales now if you're audience building. This would be considered long money. So what do we do?

The fastest way to sales is direct sales.

Do you ever wonder how multi-level marketing (MLM) companies pop up and grow so strong so quickly?

It's direct sales, and the power of in-person, relational sales. MLM's rely on their teams to connect with 100 people they know (like & trust) to purchase from them. Once the Sales Rep figures out what phone pitches or parties work, they rinse and repeat their way up the ladder. The fastest way to cash is to sell eye to eye (or voice to voice).

Take the same MLM sales rep, place them in an online setting, it will take hundreds more of people to funnel through their process to reach the same results because the "in-person" experience is absent. It takes longer to complete the full "Know, Like, Trust" cycle.

Now sales require Direct Sales. Getting your products in front of large audiences as you build your own will create the sales to get the revenue wheel moving. Depending on your product selling model & pricing strategy, wholesale is an awesome way to get larger orders quickly.

Now money's objective is to provide a quick infusion of cash, product results, and testimonials. You'll take those funds to invest in long term marketing strategies, like building audiences on social media and email marketing.

Now money also gives us time to exercise our spending muscle.

And if you're anything like me, it's hard to keep track of money going in and out when customers are constantly buying, and expenses are constantly being paid. Product sellers have a higher level of transactions than those of a service-based business. Frankly, it can be overwhelming.

Don't get me wrong, I am an advocate of having a bookkeeper, accountant, and tax expert.

But before they can do their job, we would've already spent, earned, and/or saved money generated through our business. How we use cash flowing can make or break our business.

If you haven't read Michael Michalowitz's book, 'Profit First." I highly recommend it as it simplifies how we see money, better yet, how we spend and allocate it to create a truly profitable business from Day One.

If we don't practice being a good steward when the sales are low, as the business grows or when money is funny, bills are growing, and add a dash of debt. It's easy to hold off on saving for taxes or skip paying ourselves.

"I'm going to wait till I get my next big sale or until sales are more consistent or reach $10k a month before I... [fill in the blank]" But habits die hard, so how we handle the little money determines how we handle the big money, right? So if I have a hard time putting aside 10% of $100, it's going to be that much harder for me to give 10% of $100,000, you know, $10 versus $10,000.

That's a big difference. (And we're not even talking taxes yet, lol) Disciplining ourselves at the startup season (or now. Hey, it happens.) allows us to enjoy our best sales months without worry. We're slowing down to speed up to be our most profitable ever, which means looking at how we spend our incoming sales revenue by checking how our products are priced, maximizing our networks and collaborations, getting our product sold in bulk, and always positioning our products to be seen and/or sold. These are things that we are master now to enjoy later. You know, I often talk to different eCom gurus to learn from those better than me. One of them was talking about clients making $1 million a day on Amazon.

Can you imagine making $1 million in sales on Amazon alone daily? And we hear those numbers, we think, let me jump on Amazon real quick to do the same thing.

I want to be 100% crystal clear; obviously, they did not start off that way. Open up an Amazon account, Day 1. And then two days later started making $1 million a day. That's a hard no. They put in the work in the low season, and they built up the products, customers, and sales, and they kept going, and now they're at the point where they're doing $1 million a day.

More importantly, it's how they handle the $1 million in sales that matter. Now that sales are flowing, Michalowitz's formula of assigning every dollar that flows in a task ensures your business doesn't just have vanity numbers. Looking rich, feeling poor.

No one wants that. Protect your money from yourself by assigning each dollar to one of those following accounts; Sales, Expenses, Taxes, Owners, and Cost of Goods.

As money flows into the sales account, it should flow into the remaining accounts according to the percentages your business needs to function properly.

Now, what about increasing those sales so you can exceed your goals. What can you do now?

Pause here to take action to insert some NOW money into your account.

Make or buy a list of retailers, reach out to them about your products, and begin to pitch and sell in-person or phone. Subscription boxes are the new rave for bulk sales. Again, make a list of subscription boxes, pitch, and sell. Even if they say no, continue to nurture these lists by email as you build your fan bases on social media. Once you've reached out to 100 stores or business owners, look at your conversion rate. (And not before). You'll quickly learn to adjust your pitch based on feedback received.

As money flows from direct sales, you'll pull a percentage aside to invest in your online marketing to drive more people to your website for sales.

Long money, on the other hand, sets us up for success to shift from relying on day to day sales to survive, to planning our next product launch, scaling the brand, and taking a portion of our profit to treat your staff and family with bonuses and vacations.

We're getting enough 'now' money flowing through our business, we're able to set money aside to make power moves to reach more customers, get more sales, and change more lives, selling our products, licensing our brands, creating spin-off products. Moving pallets of products on multiple platforms or finding whatever sweet spot of running your business is for you.

I remember speaking with Lindsey Laurain, Happy Mat inventor and owner Ezpz, about not wanting her company to grow into a large corporation. She wanted a small yet powerful team to reach her sales goals. Even though she was focused on sales for today (Now money), she had her eyes on the long game strategy.

Part of your long money goals is to take today's sales and reinvest into the business to grow it further. For online sales, ads will be your fastest track, but honestly, you'll need to become a student of them or use your budget to outsource it. No matter what Direction you decide, it's going to take time. Understanding the ad goals paints a better picture of the work that lies ahead.

To get high volume sales, I reached out to two ad experts to give me their take on how they would help increase traffic and generate sales. More importantly, what return on investment should we expect and work towards. One expert told me investing $1 in to get $4 is successful. Another expert told me if the ad creates a five or six dollar return on that same dollar investment that deemed successful.

Here's my take.

If you put in $1 and get $1, that ad was successful. Why? Because you've essentially bought a client, you can sell to on the back end (email marketing, FB Pixel ads, etc.) again and again. Of course, ideally, we want no minimum than a 4x Return on Investment (ROI) because we must remember our products cost something. We must replenish stock, keep the lights on in our business, pay ourselves and employees, and be profitable.

While we won't dive into ads heavily, this is why it's important to look at your products to determine what purpose they serve. Is it to trigger a customer to buy? Is it an upsell? Is it to bundle?

You'll know which products go with which ad goals and how to weight your ROI because of it.

Your long money also helps us plan for the future, inventory management, adding on more products, scaling what's already in place, and setting up our exit strategy. The planning portion of our business comes to life as we set aside funds for future activities, knowing we have consistently cash flow today.

If your eyes locked in on the term "Exit strategy" out of sheer exhaustion, you've so many sleepless nights you can't even see straight because of how much work you're doing, but your sales aren't changing fast enough. This is where we take off our superhero cape and ask for help. Free or paid.

You'll pay for free, and you'll pay for paid. Either way, your business has to grow beyond you.

When I started ScratchMeNot, I was a mom of one with a working husband. I could manage to build a business with my then small family. As the demands of the business grew, so did my family. I quickly realized I needed to automate and delegate to someone else.

DUPLICATE YOURSELF

It seemed like I could do everything with my only child by my side. I could troubleshoot customer service concerns, update the website at night, change a diaper with one hand while feeding her with another.

The next thing I knew, I was just another employee within my business. Matter of fact, several employees with very little time to be the CEO. I couldn't see it at first because my lack of children didn't shine a light on my business's flaws. As Baby #2, then #3 arrived, I had no choice but to hunker down to outsource. Not sure where your business flaws are? Want to figure out where the weak points are? Bottlenecks? Stop working for 2 weeks to go on vacation. They'll shine like the sun.

The good thing is you have experience with a lot of aspects of your business. That knowledge will make it easier for you to delegate. It's a matter of determining what to outsource first.

If you're still packing and shipping and it's eating hours of your day. Let it go (In my Frozen voice) Third-party shippers are amazing or hiring someone in house to do this laborious task for you. My kids learned how to count by helping me prep, pack, and ship my living room. Those are some of my favorite times. But the moment that topped off those was the day 40 boxes of ScratchMeNots were picked up by FedEx to allow our new shippers to send packages on our behalf.

I gained at least 15 hrs back into my work week. Whatever item is a time suck, especially non-profit-generating, outsource it or hire. You must be in tune with the heartbeat of your business, meaning if your customer service has a certain cheery sarcastic tone, handing it off to someone who is more "corporate professional" is going to change the dynamics of your brand and business. We must not forget what makes our business ours. What makes our customers engage with us? The same with social media, when sourcing support, screen, and provide a trial period to see how it works and your customers respond. Social media is probably one of the last things to delegate, but once it's done well, your brand will continue to flourish, and you'll benefit greatly.

Now about that cash infusion with NOW money. With outsourcing in place, even as you're onboarding, take a solid 2 weeks to focus on direct sales strategy approach to increase sales and brand awareness.

While your superhero cape is off your shoulders and draped over the sofa, we need to have a community of our own. For you as a business owner, mom, wife, friend, just as a busy woman.

It's time to connect with groups geared toward women entrepreneurs, product sellers, or even my own group "Get More Product Sales," where you're able to dissect just that with a mom spin on it . Knowing we may or may not have solid chunks of time to sell our products kid-free.

Matter of fact, while I'm writing this book, I have my youngest inches away. He refuses to take his feet off of me. Burnout can happen, no matter how awesome we are a business. Too many teething nights or soccer filled days can send us over the edge. The old saying goes, "we can't pour out of an empty cup."

For me, I didn't find a community until years into my business. I either met moms who were 100% momming or working moms who had 8-5 hours. It was rare I met women product sellers, drop shippers, wholesalers who understood my manic life as a mom too. Did I mention neither of our parents live close by, and it took us a while to even find a babysitter who could handle our now 5 little ones?

My point is we are all striving to grow our brand, a community to give perspective insight, suggestions, and advice. And so I would highly recommend support groups with women who take their businesses seriously and making moves. I'm an avid believer that to get where I want to be faster and without as many hurdles, be around those who are currently doing it or beyond where you want to be. And I'm not just talking business. Kids and life too.

I received so much conflicting advice from entrepreneurs about how to work with kids, put them in daycare, don't start working until they are in college, work during naps, drink lots of coffee and suck it up buttercup. It would have been AMAZING to be in a group of women who were selling products I could run ideas or questions by about the hybrid mom life and in the next breath, ask a question about business taxes.

This is why I started the 'Get More Product Sales Podcast' and Group and why circles of women exist. Building on an island equals slower growth. A community is also a place to celebrate milestones with others who understand your world with little need for explanation.

Next Steps:

The essentials of what it takes to change a massive amount of your peoples' lives have been outlined through your products. You have the Busy Mom formula. There is one thing I'd love for you tap into.

The adventure of doing life with your family, kids, and while selling more. There's always more to obtain, but what's one goal that makes you light up?

For myself, I've always wanted to live off the grid. Become a traveling homeschool family, where life is absorbed in person, and culture is observed in real-time. I looked at my husband, one day and said, "If I could hire you one day if I could retire you from your job, would you want to work with me?"

And he looked at me, and he said, "Is that even possible?" Boom! My next big goal. As a result of this goal, I would also be able to achieve 3 things in 1.

1. Showing my kids how to be an entrepreneur who sees a problem & creates a solution.
2. Reiterating to be the change you want to see in the world
3. And how to sell to make money on command.

Don't get me wrong; there's trial and error along the way, we can't avoid it all, but the reward is priceless.

It's a weird place to be, to be a working stay at home. It's a bit more challenging to connect with others because your world is a hybrid of being a working and stay at home mom, which includes running after postmen, making play-doh, and taking phone calls by day - kids homework, 137 errands and talking to a foreign country at night.

There's no need to do this alone. Join me on the inside of my community. The next legs of our journeys will be unfolding, and I'll be sharing updates & trainings inside and interviews for e-commerce successes and plunders on my podcast show. Get all the insides of

how you can surpass your goals along with resources at
www.slayecommerce.com

The fun thing about e-commerce is that everything you do is letting you know whether it's working or not. So come up for air and dive into your next 90 days to track your growth using my Busy Mom Method. Entrepreneurship challenges us to be the truest version of ourselves. It's our mirror. Similar to parenting, say whatever you want to your kids, but it's what you're doing that our kids emulate. Say whatever you want as far as your business vision & goals. But it's until you take action and follow-through with a true plan, only then will the business grow.

Simplify the way you sell, and watch your life change as you're helping others through our products.

ABOUT ANDREA

Andrea Thomas invented the Award Winning ScratchMeNot being used by children worldwide, needing protection & relief from scratching, thumb-sucking, and/or hair pulling. While giving parent's peace of mind. To this day, she continues to raise **awareness around** children's skin and allergy concerns.

As a mother of 5, she is a speaker, radio and TV guest expert encouraging women to champion their own movement to change more lives by selling more of their products. She most recently celebrated her 10,000[th] order on one of her sales channels, using her Busy Mom Method to help others simplify, grow and scale their way to increased sales.

www.ingramcontent.com/pod-product-compliance
Lightning Source LLC
Chambersburg PA
CBHW070316240526
45467CB00045B/475